It's My Turn

The Collected Radio Spots
of Don Wildmon

───── **VOLUME ONE** ─────
Edited by Rebecca Davis

American Family Association
107 Parkgate Drive
Tupelo, Mississippi 38801

© 2022 American Family Association

All rights reserved. No part of this publication may be reproduced, transmitted, or stored in whole or in part without the written permission of the publisher, except for the use of brief quotations in critical articles and reviews.

PRINTED IN THE UNITED STATES OF AMERICA
Signature Book Printing, www.sbpbooks.com

ISBN 978-1-935932-36-9

Cover design by Canada Burns

Editorial contributions by Randall Murphree and Joy Lucius

All Scripture quotations, unless otherwise indicated, are taken from the Holy Bible, New International Version®, NIV®. Copyright ©1973, 1978, 1984, 2011 by Biblica, Inc.™ Used by permission of Zondervan. All rights reserved worldwide. www.zondervan.com The "NIV" and "New International Version" are trademarks registered in the United States Patent and Trademark Office by Biblica, Inc.™

www.afa.net

Table of Contents

Foreword	7
Introduction	9
Small Deeds, Big Impacts	11
The Danger of Playing Around	13
If We Simply Listen	15
Traditions, Questions	17
Practicing Love Outshines Shouts	19
The Story of Salty	21
Just Gus	23
Emmanuel Dannan	25
Faith	29
Lord, I'm Thankful	31
Robert E. Lee	33
Seeing the Good in the Bad	35
Stinginess	37
Handling Situations	39
Working for the Thrill of Trying	41
Desire to Succeed	43
What Is Forgiveness?	45
All Things Work Together for Good	47
Power Is for Serving Others	51
Jerusalem	53
The Temple of Solomon	55
The Pool of Siloam	57
Gethsemane	59
The Young Cartoonist	63
Courage	65
In Another's Shoes	67
The Gettysburg Address	69
Responsibility Pays	71
Dynamite King	73
The Waldorf Astoria	75

Dr. A.J. Cronin	77
Before It's Too Late	79
Reaping the Harvest We Have Sown	81
True Beauty	83
Honesty Is the Best Policy	85
Jealousy Destroys	87
Not Unlike Peter	89
Christ's Journey to the Cross	91
Our Own Mount of Olives	95
The Bethany Perspective	99
The Jordan	101
The Wilderness	103
The Jericho Perspective	105
The Two Seas	109
The Samaritan Woman	111
The Nazareth Perspective	115
The Place of the Miraculous Feeding	117
The Transfiguration Site	119
The Mount of Beatitudes	121
The Adopted Home of Christ	125
Smile, Smile, Smile	127
Dropping Out of School	129
A Father's Prayer	131
Assembly Is Extra	133
I Saw God Today	135
The Boy Who Would Write	137
Everyone Has Problems	139
Two Basic Needs in Life	141
Faith. Yes, Faith.	143
What Is It You Really Want?	145

Foreword

Anyone who knows Bro. Don Wildmon understands that he has always been wise beyond his years and ahead of his time. His writings from decades ago are prophetic in the way they relate to current times.

In the early 1990s, he decided to take some of the inspirational writings he penned before American Family Association's (AFA) beginnings and turn them into brief but poignant radio spots. He titled the 3½-minute spots **It's My Turn**, and they became an instant favorite among American Family Radio (AFR) listeners.

After the initial run of the spots, they were pulled from the air for a period of time until a few years ago when they were put back on the air so Wildmon's wit and wisdom could continue to be heard. Since bringing **It's My Turn** "out of retirement," AFR and AFA have received frequent requests for the short commentaries in a print format. Thus, we're offering this first volume of 60 installments of the brief radio spots that Wildmon recorded in the early years of AFR.

"Listeners love the spots," said AFR receptionist Deanna Lineberry. "Pastors call asking for copies to share during a sermon. Listeners call wanting to hear them again so they can share with friends and family."

A Texas listener called the Tupelo flagship station and said, "There are many, many programs on AFR that are helpful to me and that I really enjoy. But the one I look forward to the most is **It's My Turn** with Don Wildmon. In those few minutes, every time I listen to him, he points me closer to the Lord."

Wesley Wildmon, AFA vice president of outreach and

grandson of Wildmon, remembers a Pennsylvania donor and listener who asked him, "When will you be making a CD or book version of **It's My Turn**?"

In another instance, a longtime AFR friend in Chicago wrote Wesley and said, "All too often, I have overlooked sending kudos to your grandpa for his amazing insight. Whether I'm home or in the car, I try my level best to catch his daily commentary, **It's My Turn**! I was home this afternoon when I caught another one. How timely and helpful are his messages for anyone at any age!"

This book project has been a long time coming, and we are excited to put Wildmon's messages of wit and wisdom into the hands of our faithful listeners. May they encourage and inspire.

Randall Murphree, editor of *The Stand* print
Rebecca Davis, associate editor of *The Stand* print

Introduction

Most people know my dad, Don Wildmon, as the founder of American Family Association (AFA). He did that in 1977. Today, AFA reaches millions of people and is a very influential ministry helping Christians be salt and light in an increasingly hostile culture. I am honored to follow in Dad's footsteps as AFA president.

Before 1977, Dad served as a United Methodist minister, led tours twice a year to Israel and Europe, wrote a column called "Whatsoever Things" that appeared in hundreds of newspapers across the country, and authored 18 books of inspiring short stories. He would send those books out to "mom-and-pop" bookstores on consignment, and those titles sold 500,000 copies. In his "spare time," he helped my mom raise four children.

My dad was a one-in-a-thousand type person. He had so many gifts and talents, and he didn't waste them. We have here the first of four planned volumes of his very best **It's My Turn** radio commentaries – brief observations on life, human nature, people, moral and social issues, cultural affairs, and most of all, spiritual truths.

Imagine these inspiring and entertaining insights and nuggets of wisdom as spoken in Dad's own voice, the voice of a rural pastor with a warm and personable delivery.

I know you will enjoy reading them and sharing them with others.

Tim Wildmon

Small Deeds, Big Impacts

It was all caused by a common house cat, investigators said. It's kind of hard to believe, but they've pieced together the events, and evidently, this is what happened. Now, listen to this. The house cat knocked a vase off of a shelf in the utility room. The vase fell onto a valve on a gas line. The impact opened the gas valve, letting the room fill with gas. Gas from the leak soon reached the water heater pilot light and ignited. The result was an explosion, which moved two walls in the house, broke windows, and started a small fire. The damage will come to about $3,000, said the news account. But luckily for Air Force Maj. James Miller and his family at Vandenberg Air Force Base in California, no one was hurt.

One never knows how far one little deed will affect his life. Things which we count as so small, so insignificant, so petty, end up dominating us. They all begin innocently enough. They're such little deeds that we hardly take them seriously. After all, what harm can such little deeds do?

Most of our major accomplishments in life start off as little things. Then they begin to grow, taking on size and importance. A person on the moon didn't start out as a big project. It started out as a little thought in the minds of people. And if you had spoken of it seriously, you most certainly would have been the talk of the town, and they would have been laughing at you. The airline industry, for instance, didn't start out the monstrosity that it is now. It started out as a thought in the minds of a few people centuries ago. And others considered those who had such thoughts, a little touched in the head.

On the other hand, most of our catastrophes didn't begin as such either. As an 11-year-old, Hitler had no dreams of murdering 6 million Jews. The idea started slowly, but it grew too fast. Nero didn't set out to be a ruler mad with insanity and jealousy, but that's the way he ended up – fiddling as Rome burned.

We don't take the little petty things too seriously. After all, they are so small. What can they hurt? Who will miss the quarter from the cash register? Surely not the company as large as it is. And soon it's a dollar the company won't miss, and soon it's a $5 bill, which the company owes me, and it ends up in what the law calls embezzlement. We fully intended to pay it back. … One social drink doesn't do any harm. It only loosens us up so we can enjoy the party. And the second helps a little more. And then another. And before long, all we want to do is to be the life of the party. Even when there isn't a party.

No person anywhere leaves that which he knows is the highest and best with one great leaping jump. Every person who betrays his Creator and himself and others does so with little things – slowly, little by little. Our lives are shaped basically by the sum total of the little things. While it may be the big things which impress us, it is the little things which influence us.

The Danger of Playing Around

Air Force Sgt. Lee Kenny has a common military habit. According to the papers, he likes to collect souvenirs for his kids. Once he happened on two bazooka type shells on the bomb range at the old Salina, Kansas, air base. He took the shells to a weapons expert to be sure that they were safe. Well, after the expert gave him the go-ahead, said they were safe, harmless, he carried the shells home with him. Kenny's two boys at home, ages 11 and 13, took a liking to the shells. They stayed around the house for about a year, and then one day the Kenny boys and some of the neighborhood children decided that they'd like to play soldier with the shells. Anybody who's ever been a young boy can recall what excitement it is to play soldier, especially if you have something related to the real soldier to play with.

The story reminds me of the fact that some things which once appeared harmful are not considered so now. Today, these are only things which many people like to play around with.

Right off the bat, I can think of alcohol. It used to be considered harmful by a great many folks. Now, society treats it as rather harmless, and a great many folks have a lot of fun playing around with it.

Then there's this thing of drugs. Many of us can remember when drugs were considered very dangerous to play around with. But today, a great number of folks, young and old alike, have found that drugs aren't nearly as dangerous as we once thought they were. And a great number are having a ball playing around with them.

Another thing which comes to mind while thinking along this line is our modern attitude toward sex. Some of us can remember when sex was considered a very wholesome and binding experience within the bond of marriage. We knew also that beyond the bond of marriage, sex could have some very dangerous consequences, or at least we thought so. But the modern-day advocates of sex have evidently proven us old fogies wrong, because everywhere we turn today, we are presented with a modern idea that sex is something to make a game of.

I guess times and people change. Some things, which at one time were dangerous, have over a period of time lost their danger and have become things for us humans to fancy ourselves with. An old war shell designed to kill and destroy over a period of time had become a toy which little boys could play and have fun with. When I read the story about Sgt. Kenny's toy shells, I thought about all of that. Even the neighborhood kids were having great fun with those old shells. Jonathan and Timothy Kellogg, ages 11 and 9. And Donald Brown and David Hasten, ages 9 and 8. They were having the time of their life playing with those old shells. They were, that is, until one of the shells exploded and killed all four boys.

Experts have taught us to change our ideas on several things. Are experts ever wrong?

If We Simply Listen

Recently, I ran across a story about a family that was eating dinner when the youngest member, a 4-year-old, stood up in his chair and blurted, "Pass the butter!" Well, that mother decided that she would have none of that. She turned to the child, spoke sharply. "You cannot have any dinner. We don't act like that around this house. You will ask for the butter politely, or you will not have any butter at all. Anyone who acts like that doesn't deserve any dinner. Go to your room immediately." The little boy started to say something, but the mother broke in: "No buts about it. Go to your room at once."

Well, most of us would agree that the child needed some discipline. No child should be allowed to stand up at the dinner table and shout like that. Children must learn, ask politely, and take their turns.

After supper, the father gathered the family together and told them he had a surprise for them. "I had the tape recorder on during the meal," he said, "and I want to play it back and have some fun. Let's just hear what we sound like while we're eating." Well, the family all gathered around and listened to the recording. Supper began on a quiet note, but before long, the group had gotten rather noisy. There was a lot of talking – loud talking and laughing. Then as the mother listened rather closely, she thought she heard something. "Go back and play that part again," she told her husband. Well, he rewound the tape and played the part she wanted to hear again, and sure enough, it was there. A very soft little voice could barely be heard beneath the noise and laughter. It spoke, "Would someone please pass the butter?" The recorder continued on and for a while all anyone could hear was the noise and the laughter. Then just a little louder than before, the voice came again. "Would someone please pass the butter?" But the noise and laughter continued. The little voice got no reply. Then it happened. The voice boomed out, "Pass the butter!" And then the voice telling him to go to his room without any supper. The mother sent for the little boy, apologized to him, and gave him his supper.

I'm afraid there are several people like that today. People who have tried to be heard in a nice way only to have doors closed in their faces and ears that would not hear. If we would have listened to the pleading of the black man years ago, perhaps our problems in race relations wouldn't be as great today. And if we had listened to the pleas of the common man, perhaps the unions would be controlled by a different breed of people today. But we were too busy with our own chatter. One of the greatest traits one can learn is to listen. You see, when we listen, it shows that we care. And after all, that's what most people want – someone to care.

Traditions, Questions

Two men who lived on tiny Haruku Island in eastern Indonesia had a disagreement. It seemed as though both of these men were rather stubborn and that each laid claim to a certain sago tree. Well, these two fellas decided to settle the question of ownership once and for all. The interesting part of the story was the method they chose to follow to decide who owned that particular sago tree. Of course, they were rather conservative. They decided to answer the question in the traditional way. By seeing who could stay under the water the longest. Now, it's true, that to us, this method seems totally unrelated to the point in question – ownership of the sago tree. But for these two men, the fact that there was no relationship between the two didn't matter. You see, tradition said that this was the way the question was to be answered, and so they answered it in that manner. Questions have always been answered this way on Haruku. And as far as they were concerned, they would always be answered in this manner.

You know, tradition is, in many respects, a wonderful thing, for tradition usually preserves that which is good. We are greatly in debt to our parents and grandparents for some of the traditions they passed on to us. We think as we think, act as we act, partly because our forefathers passed it along to us. But let us move on to add that tradition is often very damaging and demeaning. Because of tradition, slavery lasted nearly 1,900 years beyond the life of the One who came to set men free. [It was a] tradition which no one questioned, a tradition which, thank God, is broken now, but the results of that tradition still linger. Tradition has said that when two countries came to an impassable point in their differences, they went to war, and the strongest was right. Might made right.

Now, this tradition is being questioned by civilized man and rightly so. Each new generation is exactly that. A new generation. And each new generation should seek to build on the good traditions of the past and correct those traditions which we now see to be harmful to mankind.

Now, if this is a truth in the dealings of the world, then it is no less a truth in the work of the church. There are many valid and worthwhile traditions in the church, and likewise, there are traditions which need to be broken. Someone has said that the seven last words of one church were these: "We have always done things this way." Well, we don't like to change, many of us. We prefer things to remain as they are, but there's one thing certain in this world. Today is different from yesterday, and tomorrow will be different from today. And let us remember that the founder of our church broke tradition. In fact, he did so quite often. Let us therefore take the good traditions handed down to us and build on them, and let us change those traditions which are no longer valid.

If we fail to do this and hang on to tradition for tradition's sake, we could end up just like those two villagers on Haruku. You see, they both drowned. They both followed a tradition that was outdated and stupid, and they both lost. Can we expect anything different when we do the same?

Practicing Love Outshines Shouts

Occasionally, one comes across a story that speaks so loudly. There are as many stories as there are people, but they don't all come to the public's notice. One did recently. I'll let the person tell it in his own words. Having suffered a traumatic experience in childhood, he said:

"I've always had an abhorrence of funerals and dead people. When my dad died, I flew back east for the services. As I viewed his cold, lifeless body in the casket, I felt nothing. That inanimate figure bore no relationship to Pop, who had always been so happy-go-lucky and full of life. But his strengths were also his weaknesses. His carefree, devil-may-care attitude made life a constant struggle for Mom. Pop was a traveling salesman, but he was much better at traveling than he was at selling. In death as in life, he left stacks of unpaid bills. When the moment came to close the casket, my heart dropped as I saw Mom lean over and kiss him. Surely, she didn't expect me to do that. Then I heard her whisper in his ear as she had done countless times before when he had left for trips. 'Bye, Pops, I'll be seeing you.' She was sending him off on his final journey with a promise that she would join him."

The writer concluded with these words: "That gesture was a lifetime of education for me. It told me more about Mother's love for Dad than anything I had witnessed during all my years at home. I would not have missed it for the world."

You know, there are a lot of folks in this old world who carry signs and shout slogans of love. They get the headlines. And many times, few of them know very little about what they shout.

There are others who practice day in and day out what the signs and shouts say. Love causes a person to do many things, nearly all good. Perhaps those who wished to have trial marriages could learn something from the mother and wife mentioned above. Seems as though many of our modern folk have forgotten the "for better, for worse" in the marriage vows.

We've made a terrible mistake in judgment in our country. It is either the elite of society or the rags of the radicals who get the spotlight when love and marriage are mentioned. Perhaps it would help a little to shine a light on people like Mom, for it's that type person who keeps our country together. Those who stick it out through thick and thin. Those who take seriously the vows they take. Those who go on living and loving day in and day out without anybody shouting any hoorays for them.

Yes. It is the people whose love is genuine enough to carry them over the tough parts that we're indebted to. You know, love is a four-letter word, and it covers a multitude of sins and shortcomings.

The Story of Salty

Out of the papers came the story of Salty. Salty is a 21-month-old mongrel. Not an average dog, mind you, but a determined dog, nevertheless. Salty belonged to Mrs. Margie LaBeth of Detroit and was her pet. She kept Salty for some time and then gave her to some friends in the suburbs because she said, "My place is so small. I thought it wasn't fair to keep her here."

Well, the new owners kept Salty until she gave birth to a litter of puppies, and then they gave Salty to a family in Sheboygan, 272 miles northwest of Detroit. Mrs. LaBeth gave Salty away in August, and Salty stayed with a second set of new owners until around the middle of December. Then Salty suddenly disappeared. For the next two weeks, Salty traveled over 272 miles of woods, fields, streams, roads, and towns from a place where she'd never been before. And although Salty, perhaps, didn't know where she started from, she did know where she wanted to go. Home. Back to Detroit. And to Mrs. LaBeth.

On New Year's Day, Mrs. LaBeth went downstairs to take out the trash, and there stood Salty. "She knocked me down and started licking my face and kissing me," said Mrs. LaBeth. She was wet and tired and so dirty that it was difficult to tell what color she was. Her paws were bleeding, and she was starving. But with tail wagging, Salty was home. Home at last. The journey was over.

Salty set out for something she wanted more than anything in the world, and she got it. It's a story about a dog, but if you'll raise the level just slightly, you'll find the same truth about humans. We humans, like Salty the dog, usually get to the place in life where we want to go. The reason many of us never get any farther than we do is very simple. We never really want to go any farther.

I can recall the story of one man who set out to accomplish something in life. Something he wanted more than anything else. And the road that led to his dreams wasn't an easy one either. But he wanted to go, and he paid the price. Through towns where he wasn't wanted, over roads where he was spat upon, through valleys that echoed the hatred that the "good" people had for him, he traveled. When he finally arrived at the place, accomplished that which he wanted to accomplish, he was bloody and bruised and weak from a merciless beating. But he was not beaten. In his hands were huge holes caused by the metal spikes with which he was suspended on a cross. And as if that was not enough, someone slashed a hole in his side to see more blood flow.

While Salty came home dirty, tired, bloody, and shaggy, she got what she wanted – to see her master again. And the Galilean accomplished his goal too – to make it possible for us to see our Master. And because of his journey, for many of us, the journey is over.

Just Gus

Near Dublin, Ireland, an illiterate young lay preacher started a series of religious meetings in a barn. Folks who attended said it was a rather discouraging meeting. It didn't last too long. The preacher just simply stopped the services, packed up his bag, and moved on to what he considered more fruitful fields. Only a few folks turned out for those meetings, and they weren't much interested in the series. There was a young boy who had made a decision for Christ during the meetings, but no one paid much attention to him. Everybody knew him. It was just Gus, and the crowd hardly got excited when Gus made his decision.

Strange, indeed, are the ways we measure success – numbers, statistics. That's the only method many of us have to judge the worth of a venture. So we count as failures those ventures where we're not overwhelmed with numerical success. If the leading citizens of the community had come to the meetings, made decisions to become followers of the Way, well, the meetings would have been a success. They would have been continued. But just Gus, why it was as if everyone had wasted their time.

A fella told me recently that hindsight is a whole lot better than foresight. The only problem is that by the time we get to the hindsight place, we have already followed our foresight, and using our foresight, we measured the worth by the size.

I remember a story about a man who made a decision. His

townspeople didn't get too excited about it. This man decided to become a preacher. When he returned to his home church to preach, many of the people wouldn't listen to him. Do you know why? It wasn't because he didn't have anything to say worth listening to. He did, but it was because of who he was. "Is not this the carpenter's son?" they asked. And because he was the carpenter's son and not the son of the high priest, those neighbors of his would not listen to what he had to say. Instead, they literally ran him out of town following his sermon in which he spoke some unpopular truth to them.

Well, little Gus grew up and also turned out to be a preacher. He had a lot of enemies and was an enemy to some people himself. He wrote several books despite the fact that he died when he was 38 years of age. Those books are out of print now. Long since forgotten. He preached many a time, but his sermons aren't remembered now. And Gus also liked to write poems and songs. He wrote 133 in all. Most of them have not survived the years since Gus was around. But one song that Gus wrote *has* survived the years. And it gives every indication of surviving many, many more centuries. The hymn can be found in nearly every hymnbook you pick up. It is titled "Rock of Ages." It's one of the favorite hymns of millions and has been a source of inspiration to countless numbers.

Augustus M. Toplady shot a hole in the popular conception that success in a venture for the creator can only be measured in numbers.

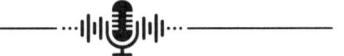

Emmanuel Dannan

Emmanuel Dannan didn't live very long, but he lived well what few years he did live. He was without parents when he was 4 years old and was placed in the Milwaukee Poorhouse. That's what they called it in those days. He spent his next three years in that institution. Then Mr. and Mrs. Samuel Norton adopted Emmanuel. The Nortons also adopted a girl at the same time they adopted Emmanuel, two years older than he. The two went to live with the Nortons on the farm in Marquette County.

Emmanuel had been living with the Nortons for about a year when Mr. Norton, whom he called Paul, told the lad of 8 to tell a lie about something. The young boy answered him back. "Paul, I don't lie." Steadfastly refusing to tell the lie that his adopted parent wanted told, Norton took Emmanuel and tied his wrist to a rafter until only his toes touched the floor. For the next two hours, Norton flogged the boy with switches while the lad kept refusing to tell the lie. When the lad was at last let down, he turned to Norton and said, "Paul, I'm so cold." That night, Emmanuel Dannan died at the age of 8, the older girl later testified in court. He died believing it was wrong to tell a lie.

Children, shameless at times, their beauty sometimes brings to light the ugliness of some of us adults. Studying human nature, one is not surprised that the carpenter took a little child, set him in the midst of the crowd, and told them that to enter the kingdom of heaven, they would have to become like that child. I have been shamed and humbled many times by the honesty and humility of children. We adults have many prejudices and hatreds, which have been ingrained in us over a period of many years. Children are free of this.

I heard a fella say once that the races should be separated among the little children because they don't know the difference. Well, like the old song says, "You've got to be taught to hate" ["You've Got to Be Carefully Taught" by Oscar Hammerstein II]. Maybe one day, adults will go on believing some of those great doctrines which they believed as children. Freedom, brotherhood, justice, love, helpfulness, kindness, appreciation, and all the others. Our world needs them far more than it needs more of the hatred and selfishness and ugliness of many of our adults.

One of the best investments we as adults can make in life is the shaping of a young mind toward that which is true in life. Those parents and teachers and friends who spend their time teaching a child to love and appreciate and be grateful do far more in preventing the destruction of the world than all the ruling bodies in the world.

Emmanuel Dannan was a great man, even if he was just 8 years old. He stayed true to the highest he knew. After he died, a fund was begun to erect a monument to the boy who would not tell a lie. A total of $1,099 was given, but the treasurer stole every penny of it. That was back in 1851. Over a hundred years later, in 1954, funds were given, and a monument was erected in Emmanuel Dannan's honor.

The Nazarene once said, "Blessed are those who are persecuted because of righteousness, for theirs is the kingdom of heaven" (Matthew 5:10). I believe I know where Emmanuel lives now. In that place, which belongs to him.

Faith

Faith. It's spoken of often but little used. And ever so few of those who use the word know the meaning of it in its fullness. What do we mean when we say the word *faith*? What picture forms in our minds? Or is it to us just a vague word without substance, which sounds good to use. What is faith? Faith goes beyond our feeble efforts to define it with words. For faith is, in reality, a complete way of life. Faith has brought to reality the highest and fondest dreams of mankind. Faith has kept many going on against tremendous odds, reaching for that which society called impossible. Faith has kept dreamers dreaming when the dream seemed to be dying.

What is faith? Again, I say it passes beyond our ability to define with mere words, but since that is the best medium we humans have, at least we should strive for something definitive on which we can build. Probably the best definition of faith ever given is this one: To have faith is to be sure of the things we hope for, to be certain of the things we cannot see (Hebrews 11:1).

The definition, of course, comes from the Book of faith. The shepherd from Nazareth never tried to give a definition of the word, but he was continually seeking to get people to live by it. Indeed, it healed a man lying paralyzed on his bed in Capernaum. It made well the sick daughter of the Canaanite woman who lived in the region of Tyre and Sidon. She was healed because of her mother's faith. And the woman who had suffered from severe bleeding for 12 years, she was healed because of her faith – faith that led her to touch the hem of his garment.

Truly he wants us to live by faith. Faith is a way of life, not merely a word. Faith is what the Maker calls us to. William Newton Clarke said that "faith is the daring of the soul to go further than it can see." And it was [Ralph Waldo] Emerson who said that "all I have seen teaches me to trust the Creator for all I have not seen."

Sure of the things we hope for, certain of the things we cannot see. The results of faith? Edwin Hubbell Chapin had this to say about them: "Skepticism has not founded empires, established principals, or changed the world's heart. The great doers of history have always been people of faith."

To try to live without faith, namely faith in a God like the Good Shepherd presented, is to fail to ever find the real substance of life. It would be like trying to be filled while eating at an empty table. I know people, with much more wisdom than I have, have given a definition for faith in the centuries gone by. And I'm sure individuals who have much more spiritual insight than I have will go on giving definitions for centuries to come. But I'm glad that it's not my lot in life to try to define it, only to experience it. And *that* we can all do regardless of our mental capacity.

Lord, I'm Thankful

Lord, I'm thankful. Today, as I was beginning my day, a friend called and said they would be happy to accept our invitation to visit our home. They are good friends, fellow workers, and their friendship means much to us. Strangely enough, I feel they need our friendship as much as we need theirs. A few years ago, they lost their only child in an automobile accident, and it's been pretty tough on them since then. For their friendship, Lord, I'm thankful.

Lord, I'm thankful. In the mail this morning came a note from a reader in Australia, the "down under" continent. He had some very kind words to say about one of the books I've written. You know, Lord, it's folks like that who keep me trying against all the odds. To know that something you do lifts another makes one feel pretty good. Lord, for the people I can help, I'm thankful.

Lord, I'm thankful. This morning, I picked up our youngest son and looked into his eyes. He's just slightly over 3 months old now, but he means so much to his mother and me. He's so precious, as all new life is. His smile makes the day so much more enjoyable. And at noon, Tim got his swimming lesson. I kept the girls while Lynda carried him to the pool. It's such a great task and responsibility, this thing of being a parent. You've entrusted to us the care and training of four wonderful children. They bring so much love and happiness to our lives. Lord, for a loving family, I'm thankful.

Lord, I'm thankful. On the way downtown, I passed by an office building where the American flag was displayed. It's symbolic of one of the greatest privileges known to mankind, this flag. For it stands for freedom, justice, service, and a host of other attributes belonging to the higher nature of man. I know that in this country, with hard work and dedicated desire, I can reach the limit of my potential. Sure, there are obstacles, but that's par for the course and makes the striving so much more exciting. Lord, for the high privilege of living in this country, I'm thankful.

Lord, I'm thankful. Today, a friend and I did a little work around the church building. My friend is such a great man in his own way. But if I ever told him, he would blush and be embarrassed. He's like many of the other folks in the church; they take their jobs as being followers of the Way seriously. And it's friends like them that keep me going when I get down in the dumps. Lord, for friends who can share with me the faith of the man of Galilee, I'm thankful.

Lord, I'm thankful. As we stopped at the light today, the family in front of us was having such a good time. They'd just bought some ice cream cones, and the mother had a double dip. One side was hers, and the other side she gave to her infant. As I sat and watched the small child enjoy that treat, I laughed out loud with joy. Lord, for the simple things in life such as a mother's love, I'm thankful.

I could go on and on, Lord. You know that. So just let me close by saying that for this day and tomorrow, and the days after, and all the wonderful possibilities they hold, Lord, I'm thankful.

Robert E. Lee

Robert E. Lee was a Southern general during the War Between the States. Most of us know that from the history books which we have read. But often the history books fail to tell us much about the personal lives of famous people. Years after the war had ended, Robert E. Lee was sitting on his porch one day in his rocking chair. The years had taken their toll on him, and his health was fast failing. While there on the porch, he was approached by two men who came from the Louisiana lottery. They came to make him a proposition. Their proposition would have made Lee a rich man.

He listened carefully as they laid out their plans, but he found it hard to believe what he heard. So Lee asked the men to repeat their offer again, thinking perhaps he had not understood their offer. Again, they made their pitch. The men didn't want Lee to invest any money; all they wanted was the use of his name for promotional purposes in their lottery. And just for the use of his name, they promised to make him rich.

Lee stood up, rising slowly. He balanced himself on his crutches. He stood erect, looked the men in the eye, and with the courage and conviction that made him great, he spoke some hot-tempered words. "Gentlemen," he said, "I lost my home in the war. I lost my fortune in the war. I lost everything I had in the war, except my name. My name is not for sale, and if you don't get out of here at once, I will hit you in the head with my crutch."

Anger. We have tended to associate it with wrong. We have forgotten that there is such a thing as righteous indignation. Holy anger. Most folks think that when you get angry, it's the devil who causes you to do so. I would guess that most of the time it is the devil who causes you to get angry. But often anger is the evidence of the love of God in one's heart.

The carpenter went into the temple courtyard one day, saw what had happened there, saw how something intended for good had been turned into something evil, and he became very angry because of it. His holy anger, righteous indignation, caused him to turn over the tables of the money changers and then gave him the courage to run some folks out of the temple. What many folks call tolerance, others call cowardice. Often, when no anger boils up within us at the sight of wrong, it is simply because we've gotten to the place where we don't care.

Wrong wouldn't stand much of a chance in our world if we could muster enough of this holy anger, this righteous indignation. Too often, we've been told that what we should do is rid ourselves of anger. What we need to learn to do is not to rid ourselves of anger, but to harness this God-given emotion, to channel it for good purposes. You see, sometimes the tables need to be turned over.

Seeing the Good in the Bad

The carpenter from Nazareth had about him some very definite human qualities, for the very simple reason that he was very definitely a human. Two of those qualities stand out. Without them, life can hardly be worth the effort of living. The first quality, which the Galilean had and which we need, is that in every bad situation he saw some good. Things must never get so dark that we cannot still see the light needed for living. It was a bad situation that Christ saw Matthew the tax collector in, but he saw the good in Matthew the man. It was a bad situation when Peter ran out on his Lord. But Jesus saw the good in Peter, even the faithfulness and steadfastness. Jesus even nicknamed him the Rock. The cross was a bad situation – man's highest contempt for God. But Jesus saw the good which could come from it.

The second quality of Jesus, which you and I need, is this: In every problem, he saw a possibility. In every problem he faced, Jesus sought and found some possibility through which he could bring honor to his Father. Faced with a problem of traveling through Samaria, a country avoided by the Jews, he used the occasion for the possibility of revealing who he was to a simple Samaritan woman at Jacob's Well. Faced with a problem of worried disciples on the Sea of Galilee in a storm, he found a possibility to show the power and concern of God.

The secret here is that we strive to be like Christ. In every bad situation, we need to look for the good. If we look for the good, we will find it. If we look for the bad or look to find fault, we'll find that. Hymn writer Thoro Harris once wrote, "Look for the beautiful, seek to find the true." No person can honestly call himself a follower of the Galilean who continually looks only for what is wrong. Jesus was a positive person who believed in the power and the goodness and the concern of God. He believed in a God who could and would help in every situation.

We also need to look for the possibilities in every problem. John Wesley, with the church doors of England closed to him, turned reluctantly to preaching in the open air. It opened a whole new, exciting, and extremely rewarding way of life to him. There's an old saying, which contains much truth: "Every adversity hides a possibility." We can actually turn bad problems into good possibilities. *Pilgrim's Progress* was written in Bedford jail where John Bunyan was a prisoner because he preached religious toleration and freedom. The famous preacher Charles Spurgeon once said that "many men owe the grandeur of their lives to their tremendous difficulties."

Occasionally, when our vision is blurred by problems, we cannot see sights which at other times are so clear. When this happens, we need more than ever to remember that the oyster turns into pearl the sand which annoys it. In every bad situation, look for the good. In every problem, seek the possibility. If you'll do these things, they will help you live and love.

Stinginess

Once while in Athens, Greece, a few of us decided to take a walk around part of that city. When we got ready to leave our hotel, an elderly lady who was in our tour group asked to go with us. We told her that we would be happy for her to come along. One of the reasons for the walk was to allow some of the other members of our group to cash some traveler's checks. So the first place we stopped was at a bank. While waiting at the bank, the lady began to tell me something about herself. She told me where she was from, who she was traveling with, and so on. Soon her conversation got around to her money. She told me how she had scrimped and saved, painstakingly looked for the best business deals, and gone without down through the years. Then she informed me that about six months earlier, she decided that since she was on up in years and that she couldn't take her small fortune with her, she was going to enjoy some of it.

You know, I thought about what that lady said. I thought of all the people I knew who made it their greatest ambition in life to make another dollar. I thought about all those people whose bankroll was larger than their spirit, whose stocks were more important than their fellow man.

Soon, some of us decided to go back to the hotel while others wanted to do some more shopping. So we split, and each person went their own way. The little lady went back with me to the hotel. Now, there was a candy shop next to our hotel, and as I started into the hotel, the lady told me she wanted to go in and get some candy.

So I went on into the hotel while she went next door to the candy shop. In the hotel, I continued to think about the lady and her conversion concerning her money. I thought about what the Galilean had to say about money and man's use of it. I thought of all the wars that had been fought, and all the murders that had been committed, and all the people who had become less than animals because of their greed for money.

Well, after a few minutes, I decided that I would go to the candy store myself and get something sweet. The little lady was still there. She was sampling every piece of candy they had, and since no one in the shop spoke English, she was having a hard time making herself understood. I could see that the salespeople were becoming annoyed with her. I found myself a piece of candy that I wanted, paid the cashier for it, and began to eat it. The lady came over, looked at my candy, and asked me if it was good. I told her that it was, and so she told the waiter that she wanted a piece of candy just like that one, the one that I had. Well, the waiter took the candy, wrapped it, and gave it to her.

"How much?" she asked. The waiter gave her the price in Greek money. She couldn't figure out the exchange rate, so she turned to me and asked, "How much is that in American money?"

I answered her, "It's 12 cents." Well, she looked at me first and then at the waiter. "That's too expensive," she said, and gave the candy back.

You know, I guess that after 50 years of stinginess, parting with 12 cents is an awful hard thing to do.

Handling Situations

At some time in his life, every person comes face to face with a difficult situation. None of us, regardless of our credentials, are spared from life's trying times. Therefore, any person is richer who has some foundation on which to stand when the storm rages high.

How can we best face difficult situations? Well, the first word that's necessary here is *dedication*. Every person has some basis from which to view life, from which he faces difficult situations. For many, that basis is pure selfishness. What's best for me? What do I want to do? For others, the basis is genuine apathy. They don't care how the difficult situation turns out.

But experience shows us that those who best cope with their difficult situations are those who have, at the center of their life, a genuinely deep and abiding faith in God. Difficult situations aren't near as difficult when a person knows that above all and beyond all is One who can and will guide us in our difficult situations. The author of the 23rd and 27th Psalms was only expressing an attitude shared by countless multitudes.

Then the second word, which is necessary here, is *decision*. Study your situation carefully. Explore all possibilities open to you. Then make the decision which seems best. It may not be the decision you desire. In many cases, that option will not be open to you, but it will be the best decision possible in a difficult situation, and that's what you're searching for. Most often our choices in difficult situations will not be between easy and hard decisions, but between hard and harder decisions. That's the reason they're difficult situations.

The difficulty comes, not so much in having a hard task to do, but in deciding the best way to do it. We can sympathize with a man who had to divide the eggs into three categories – small, medium, and large. Well, after two days, he quit, crying "decisions, decisions, decisions!" Prayer needs to be a part of our experience prior to making a decision and when facing a difficult situation. Difficult situations are hard enough in themselves, and certainly they are too hard to attempt without the help of him who has all knowledge.

The final word in facing difficult situations is *determination*. Decision should be followed by action. Else, it only amounts to indecision. Once you make up your mind to act in a difficult situation, then immediately set the wheels in motion to carry out your decision.

Perhaps the most miserable person in the world is the one who continually dwells on indecision. He will make up his mind, but he will not follow his decision with determination. He bounces to and fro, continually torn and twisted because of inaction from fear of wrong action.

In facing our difficult situations, we must always be open to new truth, new light breaking in to make the path clearer. But likewise, we must be determined to stay with the highest and best route open to us. Until that new light breaks, we must be determined to do our best in a difficult situation. In the final analysis, that's all that any of us can do in any difficult situation – our best. And when we have done that, it is good enough.

Working for the Thrill of Trying

Centuries ago, a man wrote, "I keep working toward that goal." He had not arrived, yet he continued to work at arriving. This man knew a great truth of life, a truth which kept him working at the task. Paul knew that the thrill of life is in trying. Success in life often brings satisfaction, but the thrill life offers is in trying to be successful. The thrill of life comes not from achieving our goal, but in the *attempt* to achieve it. The thrill is in trying.

Our goals in life should always be a little beyond our reach. This keeps us trying. As long as we have a goal in front of us, just a little beyond our reach, we have something to work toward. This makes life worth living. You know, life would be meaningless for me unless I had a goal that was a little beyond my reach.

Back when I first started writing, I couldn't even give my work away. I approached many publishers with a manuscript for my first book, and I'm sure a lot of them had a good laugh about it. But I wanted to write, and regardless of what others had to say, I continued to try.

Now, since that first effort, I've been able to accomplish some rather, for myself at least, good goals. But for me, the thrill is not so much in accomplishing the goal as it is in trying to accomplish that goal. Each time I nearly reach a goal I've set for myself, I push it just a little bit higher because the thrill is in trying.

We should never let the fear of failing keep us from experiencing the thrill of trying. We should never cease to try to go higher and farther because of fear; we will not make it. We will be richer simply because we tried. And also, whether we make it or not, we can experience the thrill which comes from trying.

Perhaps you wanted to do some things, but have not attempted them because you were fearful you could not accomplish them. Well, attempt them! Go at them with the best you have. Do not be afraid because you might fail. Make an effort. You will be richly rewarded, and you will also receive the thrill that comes in trying.

The thrill of following the carpenter from Galilee is in trying. You know, when you are a Christian, you're always working toward a goal which you know you will never reach. But there is a tremendous thrill in trying to reach that goal. God is continually calling us to be a little bit better, a little bit bigger than we are. Like Paul, we never arrive, but we keep working toward that goal.

The man of Galilee himself experienced the thrill of trying. The odds against him accomplishing what he attempted to accomplish and the manner in which he attempted it were infinitely great, but he was willing to try. The thrill, I say again, the thrill is in trying. "Ask and it will be given to you; seek and you will find; knock and the door will be opened to you" (Matthew 7:7). Our fondest dreams, the dreams God has planted in our hearts, can come true, and the thrill of life is in trying to make them come true.

Desire to Succeed

There is within each of us a desire to be a success in life. It is a desire which God placed within us. Too many of us find our efforts toward success frustrating. This need not be the case. Success is indeed within reach of every person.

One way to succeed, and by far the easiest, is *to never try*. Now, that statement may seem a little strange, but if you'll study it for a moment, you will see the validity of it. Never attempt anything, and you will never fail. Success will be automatic, even guaranteed. The world is full of people who never tried. They set their goals so low that they could not miss. They achieved their success early and easy.

I knew a man once who was a great success, at least in his own eyes, as a member of his church. He came and joined and never came back until his funeral. He set his goal low and reached it quick and easy. It takes no great effort to succeed when one's goal is low, and a person can pat himself on the back while commending himself for great success. You'd be surprised at the number of people who have followed this easy route to success.

But still another way to be successful is *to try half-heartedly*. This is, of course, the best route open to those who wish to get out cheap while maintaining their self-respect. They can say, "I tried," and they did do that. They tried. They succeeded in trying. There were those who laughed at Thomas Edison when he began working toward developing an electric light. They told Edison that it couldn't be done because they had already tried it, and they had. And for the most part, they were well-respected men in their profession and well educated. But they laughed at Edison, but Edison wasn't satisfied with a half-hearted effort. He set his goal a little higher.

Now, the third route toward success is *to be serious*. It was said once by John Mark concerning Jesus that when someone made a certain remark to the Galilean, that he, quote, "paid no attention to them." What a grand statement! What a terrific statement! When those about him were trying to get Jesus to lower his goals, his ideals, his ambitions, he paid no attention to them. The person who is serious about success will pay no attention to the prophets of doom. Now, this path toward success isn't easy and is often very disappointing. It is difficult sometimes to keep our goals high and not listen to the words of the world. People laughed at Edison, called him a fool for trying seriously, but they don't laugh at him now when they flip the light switch People also laughed at Christ, but only foolish people laugh at him today.

The all-important question is this: What do we mean by success? Success by whose standards? God is the final judge over our success. And often we may be a failure in everyone else's eyes except his. When a person has done the best he can do and remained true to the best he has known, then in God's eyes, he is a success. That's the reason I say that success is within reach of everyone … even you.

What Is Forgiveness?

The Bible contains the story of David and Bathsheba. Bathsheba was the very beautiful wife of Uriah, a soldier in David's army. David's desire for Bathsheba was so great that David arranged for Uriah to be in the front charge of the next battle, where the chance of his death would be great. Well, after Uriah died fighting for David, David took Bathsheba to be his wife. When David's preacher, Nathan, confronted him with this evil deed, David longed for forgiveness. You will find in Psalm 51 David's cry for forgiveness.

What is forgiveness? What is this thing David longed for? Well, forgiveness is a cleansing of the soul. "Create a pure heart in me, O God," was David's plea (Psalm 51:10). Forgiveness is a clean heart. It was the prophet Isaiah who said, "Though your sins are like scarlet, they shall be as white as snow; though they are red as crimson, they shall be like wool," (Isaiah 1:18). Forgiveness is becoming clean in our heart.

William Cowper, the English poet, expressed quite beautifully what forgiveness is. These are the words he penned: "There is a fountain filled with blood drawn from Emmanuel's veins; and sinners, plunged beneath that flood, lose all their guilty stains."

Now, the next question is this: How can one receive forgiveness? The answer is basically quite simple. First, one must forgive those who have wronged him. This is necessary to get his heart conditioned for forgiveness. Then, all that is necessary to receive forgiveness is to ask for it. Now, it may seem strange that the prerequisite for forgiveness to be received is that forgiveness must be given. But such is the case. Jesus taught, "For if you forgive other people when they sin against you, your heavenly Father will also forgive you. But if you do not forgive others their sins, your Father will not forgive your sins" (Matthew 6:14-15). The best way one can get even with another who has wronged him is to forgive.

Forgiveness may seem a strange way to get even. But if you doubt the wisdom of the statement, then try it. There isn't enough room in your heart for both revenge and love. One of them will have to go. Give love a chance, and it will drive revenge out.

Several years after his affair with Bathsheba, David was seriously wronged by his son Absalom, but David was quick to forgive his son. Perhaps the reason that David forgave Absalom so quickly was that he had already experienced God's forgiveness.

You know, guilt can weigh heavy on a person's heart. It can cause him no end of anxiety and worry. It can severely tax the physical health of the human body. But the good news is that there is a release from guilt. There is a place where we can deposit our guilt and leave it. And that place is with God. If you want forgiveness, first of all, forgive those who have wronged you. Then ask for God's forgiveness in a sincere way, and forgiveness is yours. Just remember that the only sin for which you cannot find forgiveness is the sin which you fail to ask forgiveness for.

All Things Work Together for Good

There is in the book of Romans a sentence which reads like this: "And we know that in all things God works for the good of those who love him, who have been called according to his purpose" (8:28). Now, are those just some fancy sounding words Paul is using? Is this just some good prose, or are they true? Does God work for good in everything with those who love him? Does God use even the bad things that happen to those who love him when he's working for good?

I feel we need a little background on Paul before we can get his statement in proper perspective. You see, he had been a Christian for 22 years. He was making preparations to go to Spain. That was his heart's desire. History would record that he got only as far as a Roman jail cell. Paul had suffered much prior to pinning these words. Five times he had been whipped with 39 lashes from a leather whip tipped with metal. He had been beaten with rods three times. He had been stoned once, left for dead. He had been in three shipwrecks. He had suffered from heavy toil and hardship and had spent many sleepless nights and who knows how long in jail. After suffering all of this and more, Paul wrote that God works for good in everything for those who love him. At least Paul was speaking with plenty of experience, and you can put this down: Paul believed what he wrote.

But back to the original question: Does God work for good in everything with those who love him? Events in the life of Christ add validity to Paul's statement. For we are told that God took mankind's most evil and unjust act, the crucifixion, and worked good through it. After a study of the evidence available, one comes to the conclusion that Christ shared this belief with Paul: that God works for good in everything for those who love him.

Does God work for good in everything? May I share with you a personal experience? Back when I started preaching, I served a little rural church. Since the church didn't pay much, couldn't pay much, Lynda taught school to help pay our bills. We gave very liberally to the little church. Probably more than any other family. We thought nothing about it. We did it because we wanted to do it. When Lynda had to give up her teaching because of pregnancy, we cut our expenses every way we could. I was in seminary then, and the bills seemed just to keep piling up. In order to help pay our hospital bill, I did something I had never done before or since. I asked the church to raise my salary $20 a month for four months.

I explained that the money was needed to help meet our hospital expense. There was sufficient money in the church treasury to meet the request without affecting the church's finances. But the church denied my request. I can recall that as I heard the decision that night, that it just didn't make sense. We had worked so hard for that little church, given so generously when we could. Now, when we needed just a little help, the church said no.

You know, I can remember that I was unable to finish my sermon that night. For the first time in my life, I cried in a church. I could not hold back the tears; I was deeply hurt. But God worked good from that. For I learned how to be a little more loving and kind, a little more understanding and helpful. Because of that deep hurt, I know something of what the other fella feels when he hurts.

And perhaps I learned a little of the hurt in the heart of God when we say no to him. Does God work for good in everything? I believe he does. I believe that even in our disappointments and heartbreaks, God is working for our good.

Power Is for Serving Others

In the Bible, we have the story of Jesus stooping to wash the feet of his disciples. This was a very unusual act for Jesus to do. For it was not the task of the master to wash his servants' feet. Rather, it was the responsibility of the servant to wash the feet of the master. It was such an unusual action that one of the disciples, Peter, was not going to let Jesus wash his feet. No way was he going to let Jesus wash his feet! But Jesus would have it no other way. You know, there are three tremendous truths we can gain from this incident.

First of all, this incident shows the *purpose of power*. Just what is that purpose? You know, it's an ageless question. Well, the purpose is not to rule, as many think. Someone once said, "Every man would like to be God, if it were possible; some few find it difficult to admit the impossibility." Remember Hitler or Caesar and Nero? Neither is the purpose of power to force, despite what some people think. A very wealthy businessman once made this statement. He cursed the people, and then he said, "I have the power. I have the power." Many share that attitude.

The purpose of power is to serve. Christ illustrated this so magnificently when he stooped to wash the feet of his disciples. Despite the belief to the contrary, there is more power in the open hand than in the clenched fist. "All power is given unto me," Jesus said (Matthew 28:18, KJV). What did he do with that power? He served.

This incident also shows the *goal of greatness*. Again, the question surfaces. What is the goal of greatness? Why do we all, in our own way, seek greatness, and after we achieve it, what do we do with it? Two disciples, James and his brother John, once asked Jesus for the preferred places in heaven. When the other 10 became angry, that is the other 10 disciples became angry, Jesus told them, if any one of you wants to be great, you must be the servant of the rest (Mark 10:43). Now, that is the goal of greatness. The goal of greatness is not to separate one from the lowly, poor, and needy as fame and fortune so often do. Neither is it to exalt one to a position superior to your fellow man. But the goal of greatness is to serve. The greatest one is the one who serves most. The goal of greatness is service. Stephen Grellet once wrote, "I shall pass through this world but once. Any good, therefore, that I can do or any kindness that I can show to any human being, let me do it now. Let me not defer it or neglect it, for I shall not pass this way again."

This story of Jesus washing the feet of his disciples also shows the *height of humility*. This one who had all power and greatness knelt and washed the feet of his servants. "All authority in heaven and on earth has been given to me," he said, yet he stooped to wash their feet (Matthew 28:18). Jesus put himself into the role of a servant. "Those who humble themselves will be exalted," he said (Luke 14:11). How odd those words seemed back then, even more so today. But who do we exalt today? Hitler, Caesar, Napoleon, Nero, or the lowly Christ? Go after power. Nothing wrong with that. Get it, but use it right: to serve. Go after greatness. Get it, but use it right: to serve. And remember that if a person wants to grow tall, he must bend low. For without humility, nothing else fits in place.

Jerusalem

In the book of Psalms, we read these words: "If I forget you, Jerusalem, may my right hand forget its skill. May my tongue cling to the roof of my mouth if I do not remember you, if I do not consider Jerusalem my highest joy" (137:5-6).

Jerusalem is located some 33 miles east of the Mediterranean Sea and some 14 miles west of the Dead Sea. For some 25 to 30 centuries, it has been a holy city. Today, it is a center of three major religions: Judaism, Islam, and Christianity. It is a city well known to millions of Bible readers. David and Solomon lived in this city. So did Isaiah and Jeremiah and a host of other Old Testament figures. It was in this city that Stephen became the first Christian martyr. Also in this city, James, the brother of John, died at the hands of Herod Agrippa I about A.D. 44. Agrippa was the grandson of Herod the Great.

The city is literally covered with biblical landmarks. Some are authentic. Some are marked only by legend and tradition. The Dome of the Rock, a Muslim mosque, is a distinguishing mark in the city. It is constructed on the site of Solomon's Temple and over the rock where Abraham is supposed to have offered Isaac as a sacrifice. Always in Scripture, those who went to the city were going up to Jerusalem. This is true for two reasons. The city is located on hills at a height of some 2,600 feet above sea level. So the journey was a physical trip up, but more than this, Jerusalem was considered the most holy city in the world. So then it was also a spiritual journey up to the city. The best view of the city is offered from the Mount of Olives. Standing atop this mountain and looking across the Kidron Valley to the city, one can see reminders of centuries of biblical history. In fact, every place associated with the last week in the life of Christ is visible from the Mount of Olives.

Jesus came to this city often. His first visit was as a baby, perhaps slightly more than a month old. His last visit was probably just prior to his ascension. In the temple courtyard, located immediately east of the present Dome of the Rock, he taught the crowds. In Jerusalem, he ate the Last Supper with his disciples. It was here that he was arrested, tried, and crucified, and it was here that he arose from the dead. The name of the city means City of Peace. It is misleading. For throughout its history, the city has known very little peace. It has been destroyed and rebuilt many times. Perhaps the most famous destruction was that by Titus, the Roman general in A.D. 70. That destruction was prophesied by Jesus some 40 years earlier.

Pilgrims by the multitude still flock to the city. They come from every race and every nation. Many of them have one thing in common. They are followers of the Christ who visited here, and they have come to see places made universally famous by the one they follow.

The Temple of Solomon

"Then Solomon began to build the temple of the Lord in Jerusalem on Mount Moriah, where the Lord had appeared to his father David. It was on the threshing floor of Araunah the Jebusite, the place provided by David" (2 Chronicles 3:1).

You know, the temple played a significant part in the life of Christ. It was located, of course, in Jerusalem. It was here and here only that sacrifices could be offered. The original temple was conceived in the mind of King David. However, it was his son, Solomon, who constructed the First Temple. Solomon began construction of the temple in 960 B.C. The temple became the religious center for world Jews.

Actually, in the Bible, not one, but three temples are mentioned. Solomon's Temple was destroyed by Nebuchadnezzar II about 587 B.C. Another temple was constructed by Zerubbabel in 516 B.C. This temple was no comparison to the original structure and was frowned upon by those old enough to remember Solomon's Temple. Zerubbabel's Temple was destroyed and later replaced by Herod the Great's magnificent structure. Herod completed the sanctuary area of the temple in 19 B.C., after 18 months of construction. However, the buildings in the temple area took more than half a century to complete. Construction on Herod's Temple was continuing during the life of Jesus. The building was completed only a short time before it was destroyed by Titus in A.D. 70. It was never to be rebuilt.

Jesus visited the temple often. His visits began shortly after his birth and continued until the week of his death. On one visit, when he was 12 years of age, he became separated from his parents while visiting the temple. In the temple area, he taught, and like an unpopular preacher, he minced no words in his exhortations. In this area also, he healed the blind and the lame. His popularity with the people here offended the chief priest and the scribes.

Nothing remains of the temple in Jerusalem today. Only a section of the wall which surrounded the temple area still stands. Today, it is known as the Wailing Wall. The Jews come here to weep over the destruction of their temple. Ancient legend says angels came and sat on this wall and wept when the temple was being destroyed. It is the most holy site in the world to the Jewish people.

Prior to the destruction of the temple by Titus, Jesus had spoken of its ruin. He had stated that not a stone would be left unturned. When the temple burned, the precious metal melted and ran between the cracks of the structure. Later, scavengers searching for that precious metal turned over every stone. The words Jesus spoke were true. Jesus knew the value of the temple. He knew the value of people coming together to worship. There's always the need of people to come together and share in worship. "No man," as John Donne said, "is an island," and while we don't have a temple, we do have a church. If Jesus felt the need to attend the temple services, surely, we need to attend the services of our church.

The Pool of Siloam

"After saying this, he spit on the ground, made some mud with the saliva, and put it on the man's eyes. 'Go,' he told him, 'wash in the Pool of Siloam' (this word means 'Sent'). So the man went and washed, and came home seeing" (John 9:6-7).

The Pool of Siloam is to be found in the southeastern section of Jerusalem. Today, it is outside the walls around the old city. In the time of Christ, it was inside the city walls. In fact, it was the water source for the city in time of attack. King Hezekiah, seeking a water source for use by the city under attack, cut a tunnel some 1,750 feet from the spring of Gihon to the pool. The tunnel was cut through solid rock in order to bring water inside the city walls. The tunnel was one of the most amazing engineering feats for water supply in the biblical period.

Two groups of workmen began at opposite ends and worked toward the center. Using hand picks, the two groups dug in a zigzag pattern. The pattern resulted in a tunnel 1,750 feet in length to cover a distance of only 1,100 feet.

In 1880, two boys were wading in the tunnel when one accidentally discovered an inscription carved in the rock. The inscription was located about 19 feet from the Pool of Siloam. The inscription, one of the oldest Hebrew inscriptions known, contained only six lines. They were beautifully cut in classical Hebrew. The inscription told how the two groups managed to meet in the middle. The slab containing the inscription is today preserved in a Turkish archaeological museum at Istanbul.

The pool's name, Siloam, meant "sent." The name is symbolic of the water being sent through the tunnel into the city. The pool is an open-air basin and measures only about 20 by 30 feet today.

It was to this Pool of Siloam that Jesus sent the man who had been blind since birth. You will recall that John makes no mention of the man requesting his sight, but after Jesus spat on the ground and made mud, which he applied to the man's eyes, Jesus told him to go wash in the pool. The man did as he was told. It was here in the clear, clean water that the man born blind first saw what he looked like.

The religious authorities called the man in to question him about the event. After much questioning and debate, the authorities attempted to pin the label of sinner on Jesus. The healed man would not get involved in their theological arguments. He presented his case by speaking what he knew was fact: "Whether he is a sinner or not, I don't know. One thing I do know. I was blind but now I see!" (John 9:25).

You know, you can't argue with that. Just prior to the healing of the man, Jesus had said to him, "I am the light of the world ..." (John 8:12). After he could see physically, the man again came into contact with Jesus. And so for the second time, Jesus healed him of his blindness. For on the second meeting, Jesus healed him of spiritual blindness. Many who visit the Pool of Siloam today recall that event recorded by John in his Gospel. And they also are able to say, "Once I was blind, but now I see."

Gethsemane

"Then Jesus went with his disciples to a place called Gethsemane, and he said to them, 'Sit here while I go over there and pray'" (Matthew 26:36).

Gethsemane is located in a valley. Perhaps that is symbolic, for life cannot be lived on mountaintops. It is a series of highs and lows. And here at Gethsemane was a low period for our Savior. Gethsemane is located in the Kidron Valley between the Mount of Olives to the east and the temple area inside the walls of Jerusalem to the west.

It was a favorite spot for Jesus, and no doubt he came here often to pray and rest. On the night of his arrest, he had brought with him his disciples. Three of them – James, John, and Peter – he took on into the garden. He went farther into the garden to pray, asking a simple request of his three friends – that they watch for him while he prayed. But three times he returned to find them sleeping. Perhaps because it was late and they were tired, or perhaps because they did not understand the seriousness of the situation.

It was in Gethsemane that Jesus agonized in prayer. His will came into conflict with God's will. He could see before him an ugly and painful cross, which he wished to avoid. The sight and smell of blood from the slaughter of sheep for the Feast of the Passover flowing in the nearby Kidron Brook was heavy that night. No doubt the aroma brought to his mind the very likely possibility that his blood would flow in a very short time. Jesus was not in that garden very long until he noticed a small group of Roman soldiers and Jewish temple guards, led by Judas Iscariot, coming toward the garden. Down the steps, which passed by the home of Caiaphas, the high priest, they came. The very same steps Jesus and his disciples had walked down after leaving the Upper Room.

Upon arrival, Judas greeted Jesus with a kiss – the traditional greeting among friends. "Master," cried Judas, as he kissed Christ. How many times since then he has endured the same type of hypocrisy! They carried him away from Gethsemane to a fate no person should have to endure. He went willingly because he had decided while praying in the garden that God's will and not his would prevail. Perhaps as they walked away, he looked up to the Golden Gate across the Kidron Brook and remembered the previous Sunday's events, when the crowd cried, "Hosanna!" There was no crowd other than the soldiers now and no hosannas – only silence and darkness.

The garden of Gethsemane is still there in the Kidron Valley today. This place of the wine press has eight olive trees growing in it. They're snarled and twisted from age. Looking at them, one is reminded of the terrible agony Christ experienced here. It's never an easy matter to do the will of God, and every person who tries will eventually come to Gethsemane. Some continue in his way from Gethsemane. Others turn back and walk with him no more.

Gethsemane is located in a valley. It always will be. For the crucial decisions which life places upon our shoulders are never decided on a Mount of Olives. The crucial, real, life-directing decisions come when we are in the valley, and this is as it should be. For the person who believes in God in the darkness of the valley is the only person who believes in God at all.

The Young Cartoonist

There was this young boy once. He loved to draw. He'd take a pencil and a piece of paper, and he'd draw anything around him that caught his fancy. Once that young boy was asked by an elderly gentleman to draw a picture of a horse. When he'd finished with the drawing, the gentleman was so pleased with the boy's work that he gave him a whole dollar. Now, that was back when a dollar was a dollar. That seemed to spur the youngster on. He kept drawing. He worked at it. He loved it. He gave himself to it. Soon he had landed himself a job with a newspaper as a cartoonist. Now, he was real proud of himself when he got that job, but while he thought it was something to get excited about, one of his superiors didn't see it that way.

The editor of the paper where he worked in Kansas City called him in one day, said he wanted to talk to him about his future. He was quite frank with the young cartoonist about his job and about his future, and he said to him: "You don't have any talent; why don't you get out of the drawing business and into something where you have a chance to succeed?"

Well, the young fella thought it over. Gave some serious consideration to doing just that, quitting his drawing and going into another line of business. For like most of us, he did want to be a success, and the editor should have known something about talent, he thought. But after considerable thought, he decided to stay in the drawing business, even if he didn't have any talent.

You'll find people like that occasionally. People who won't quit. People who won't give up, even if others think they are doomed to failure. No one has ever found the magic formula that separates those who refuse to quit from those who give up at the first setback. A lot of time, however, it can be nothing more than the spirit of God driving them on. For sometimes, there's not a single person in this whole world who believes in us other than him. That's one of his traits. He believes in us even when no one else does. He believes in us, even when we don't believe in ourselves. That's what made him face that ugly cross. He believed in our goodness when we displayed our sinfulness. He never gave up on us. He still is counting on us to this very day. He's disappointed a lot of times, but he never gives up. When everyone else has counted us out, he's still pulling for us.

Oh, by the way, that young artist who had no talent but wouldn't quit? He went on to pretty great things. His name was Walt Disney. No one can remember the name of the Kansas City editor.

Courage

A woman's scream suddenly startled a party of surveyors in a forest in northern Virginia on a calm, sunny day in 1750. The men ran in the direction of the scream. One of the first to reach the scene was an 18-year-old. "Please, sir, please make them release me," the woman said, as several held her. "My boy is drowning, and they'll not let me go to save him."

One of those holding her yelled, "It would be madness. She'll jump into the river and drown herself." Well, the young man threw off his coat, sprang to the edge of the bank, scanned for a moment the rocks and whirling currents, and then, catching a glimpse of the boy, plunged into the roaring rapids. "Thank God," the mother said. "He will save my boy."

Everyone watched as the young would-be rescuer fought the rocks and the whirlpools. Twice the rescuer disappeared from sight only to come back. He was nearing the part of the river that was most dangerous. The rush of the waters was so dangerous at that spot that no one had ever dared approach it, even in a canoe. And into the middle of it, he went. Finally, he grabbed the boy, lifted him above the water with his strong right arm, but at that moment, those standing on the bank cried in horror. Both the youth and the child shot over the falls and vanished into the waters below. Following a deadly few seconds, the mother shouted, "There they are! See, they're safe!" Soon, the youth, exhausted, and the boy, senseless, reached the bank. The friends were there to meet them. "God will give you a reward," solemnly spoke the grateful woman. "He will do great things for you in return for this day's work, and the blessings of thousands, other than mine, shall be yours."

You know, we call it courage. That thing that made the youngster do what he did. When others refused, were afraid, called it hopeless, he jumped into the water without thought of any danger he faced. One thing raced in his mind above everything else: Another human needed help.

Courage is a wonderful thing. It's something that you don't normally get overnight. You have to work at it, make it a way of life. The carpenter had it too, you know. He was a man who inspired others with his courage. When they threatened him with bodily harm, he stood fast. When they gave him a choice between a lie or a cross, he chose the cross and truth. Oh, I nearly forgot that the woman's prediction about the young man, it proved correct. Some 39 years later, he was installed as the first president of the new country called the United States of America. His name was George Washington.

In Another's Shoes

There was a boy once; he happened to be the son of a very well-to-do father. He wore nice clothes, lived in a nice house, and ate very good food. One day, this young boy happened to get into a scuffle with another boy who lived on down the street. The other boy came from a poor family, lived in a cheap house, wore ragged clothes, and had less than the first boy to eat. In the scuffle, the rich boy threw the poor boy and was the winner. In a few moments, the poor boy got up, dusted himself off, and said that if he had food to eat, like the rich boy had, he could throw the rich boy. The poor boy turned and walked away, but the rich boy stood there. He was numbed by what the poor boy had said. His heart was broken because he knew quite well that what the poor boy had said was true.

The rich boy never forgot that experience. From that day on, he revolted against any favored treatment because he was rich. He made it a point to wear cheap clothing like the poor wore. He intentionally endured the hardships that the poor faced. His father was often embarrassed by the way he dressed, but despite all the urging to act like he should, that young boy never again took advantage of his wealth.

Back several hundred years ago, there was a man who said something like this: "I sat where they sat." In other words, he put himself into the suffering and misery endured by others, and by so doing, he could feel what they felt, experience what they experienced, hurt when they hurt. That man's name was Ezekiel (Ezekiel 3).

The Indians in this country had a saying that fits into this same theme. It went something like this: "Never criticize another brave until you have worn his moccasins for seven moons." And we Americans have a saying about wearing another man's shoes. I have an idea. We might need to do a little of this. To wear the other person's shoes for a while. Far too often, we're too hasty to pass judgment, condemn a person for something, when we don't know all the facts. How many of us have had to wear the shoes of a poor boy? How many of us have had to face life with skin a different color than the majority? How many of us have seen our children go hungry, cold, and ignorant simply because it wasn't their lot to be born into the "right" family?

Maybe if we would sit where they sit, face what they face, endure what they endure, we would be surprised how much they need our help, instead of our cutting, cruel criticism. If I remember correctly, this is one reason the Galilean came. How was it said? "For we do not have a high priest who is unable to empathize with our weaknesses, but we have one who has been tempted in every way, just as we are – yet he did not sin" (Hebrews 4:15). He has sat where we sit. He understands. Maybe that's the reason he can help us. The young boy who won the fight went on to give his life to the poor. He became one of the world's most famous men. His name was Albert Schweitzer.

The Gettysburg Address

On November 19, 1863, two men were speakers at the dedication of a soldier's cemetery on a famous battlefield in Pennsylvania. One of the men who was to speak was the main speaker for the day, and the other had only a few words to say. The man who spoke first, the featured speaker, spoke for a full two hours. The other gentleman said what he had to say in three minutes and used only 219 words to say it.

Two years later, both of these men were dead. The featured speaker died as a result of natural causes. The man who had only a few words to say died as a result of an assassin's bullet. Very few people have ever heard any part of the featured speaker's address. Yet nearly every school child in America has learned by heart the words of the second speaker.

I guess as one looks back at it, how much one says isn't all that important. Now, you preachers and politicians, you need to take note of what I'm saying. One is left with a firm impression that what matters most is *what* one says. In other words, it isn't quantity that counts in the long haul, but quality. And this principle could be applied not only to speeches, but more specifically to lives.

Take the example of the life of Frederick William Robertson. There is hardly a person who has studied at the job of being a minister, who has not only heard of this man but also studied his writings. He was the pastor of Holy Trinity Church in Brighton, England. He regularly preached to larger crowds than most preachers do today. His sermons have been preserved and printed, yet he died when he was only 37 years old.

Or consider Nathan Hale. He was a schoolteacher prior to the Revolutionary War. Entering the service, he was commissioned a captain. He volunteered for spy duty behind the lines of the enemy, knowing the penalty should he be captured. He was captured and was hanged the next day. The enemy refused his request for a Bible and the services of a minister. Yet he died only after saying that he regretted that he had only one life to give for his country. He was dead at the age of 21.

There was another who lived only a short time. He was a carpenter until he was about 30 and then turned to preaching. His ministry was extremely short, covering a period of approximately three years. He enjoyed moments of popularity and acceptance as a minister and a pastor and a preacher, but was eventually rejected and put to death as a criminal, an enemy of the state. His name was Jesus of Nazareth. He died at the age of 33.

The two men who spoke at Gettysburg that day in 1863 were Edward Everett and Abraham Lincoln. I don't have to tell you which man's speech is remembered because most of us know the Gettysburg Address.

Responsibility Pays

Back more than a hundred years ago, a father gave his son sufficient money with which to attend college until he earned his diploma. The father told his son that this was all the money he was to have. Said that if the son spent it wisely, it would be more than enough for him to graduate from college. The young boy took the money and went off to school. At the end of the first year, he returned home and told his father that he'd spent all the money and needed more in order to return to school. To the young man's surprise, his father refused to give him another penny. He told him that he'd already given him plenty of money to go to college on and that there would be not another penny forthcoming.

Stunned, the boy found that all the props had been removed from beneath him. While living it up in his freshman year, he never thought that his father would refuse to give him more money. His father had it, and he was going to have a good time on it. But now the money source was gone. He had to sink or swim totally on his own merits.

There are many who would criticize the father for his action. In today's modern society, there are those who would claim that the father's action would destroy the boy's personality and that he should continue to support the boy no matter what he did. Other folks would defend the boy's right to more money on educational grounds that the boy had a right to seek his own education as he saw fit.

I guess for a large number of folks today, the father's action was totally wrong. They send their kids off to school and continue to supply the funds no matter what Junior does or what grades he makes. They blame the teachers if Junior flunks the course and blame the establishment if he gets caught breaking the rules. "Junior isn't wrong," they cry, "but the rules are. The rules should be changed to protect Junior."

Divinely implanted in each person is a desire to be a responsible person. We're made that way. Sometimes it's necessary to face the worst, even a cross, in order to bring out the best.

Somehow, I have an idea that the young boy's father took a signal from a higher power. For our Creator tells us there are certain laws that we're to live by, and if we break them, then we must be prepared to pay the penalty. Often as we have to pay the penalty, we become responsible citizens in his world.

Well, the young boy went back to school without any money. Worked his way through, graduated at the head of the class, studied law, was elected governor of the state of New York, and became the secretary of state during the Civil War. He was later responsible for the purchase of some land, which many dubbed Seward's Folly. Today, the folly is known as Alaska. The young boy's name was William Seward. His father's discipline saved him from a possible life of wastefulness. You know, maybe discipline isn't so bad after all.

Dynamite King

Over in Sweden one morning, late in the 1800s, a fella woke from his sleep to find himself dead. Well, not really dead. It was just that the newspapers had gotten him confused with his brother. And when they printed the obituary, they had printed his by mistake.

Imagine that! Reading your own obituary. Talk about a shocking experience! Well, it was a really shocking experience for this particular fella. For the first time in his life, or death as it appeared, he saw himself as others saw him. It seems that the reporter in writing the obituary referred to him as the Dynamite King. You see, this man who had supposedly died had spent his entire life in the field of explosives. He had discovered dynamite, blasting gelatin, and ballistite along with detonators for explosives. In the process, he had grown extremely rich, and now, with the world thinking he was dead, he didn't like what he was being remembered for.

This fella didn't like the idea of being remembered as the Dynamite King. To him, the nickname implied something that he thought was destructive. So at that very moment, he set about to correct the situation. He took his money and put it into a trust fund to promote awards for people who had contributed the most good in particular areas of man's concern each year. He set up five areas including physics, chemistry, physiology or medicine, literature, and peace. The winner of the award in each area annually receives gifts of money for his efforts.

You know, I guess many of us would change a few things if we knew what the world would remember us for. Most of us are like the fella mentioned earlier. We are of the opinion that when we die, people will pay tribute to us for our great gains or our hard work. A lot of us would be just as surprised as he was if we could read our own obituary, if we could see what we would be remembered for. One of the real mistakes we humans habitually make is that of thinking more highly of ourselves than we ought to.

[The apostle Paul] had something to say about that a few hundred years ago. He said we should think of ourselves with sober judgment. What he knew is that many times we drink until we are drunk with our own pride, selfishness, and ego. What am I doing that I'll be remembered for? If a lot of us would spend the next 10 minutes answering that question in sober judgment, it could bring about just as tremendous a change in our lives as it brought about in the life of the gentleman mentioned earlier.

He changed for the good. A lot of us need to do that also. If you're wondering about who the man was, his name was Alfred Bernhard Nobel. If you have never heard of him, you may have heard of the Nobel Prizes. Those are the awards he established as a direct result of reading his own obituary.

The Waldorf Astoria

Back many years ago, an elderly couple – a man and his wife – were passing through Philadelphia. Being tired and the night half gone, they searched for a hotel where they could get some rest. Every hotel they went to told them the same thing. "Sorry, we're filled up." Finally, in desperation, the couple tried a little third-class hotel. As they entered the hotel, the man went to the night clerk and said, "Mister, please don't tell me you haven't got a room. We've searched all over town for a room, but the conventions have filled up our usual hotels. We're so tired. Please don't tell me that you don't have a room where we could get some rest."

The night clerk looked at the couple, saw how tired they were, and then said, "I'm so sorry, sir, but our hotel is completely full." The expressions on the couple's faces turned to disappointment. They turned, started to walk out. Then the night clerk spoke again. "Sir," he said, "I have a room which I'll not be using tonight. I have the night shift and will be working all night. It isn't a fancy room, not as nice as the others, but it is clean. And if you wish, I would be happy for you to be my guest for tonight."

Well, their faces lit up with gladness. Their disappointment was turned to happiness. The woman said, "God bless you, young man." Feeling like a million dollars, the clerk showed them to his room. Next morning, the couple went to eat breakfast. At the table, they sent the waiter to get the night clerk. They sent a message [that] they wanted to see him. Entering the room, the clerk spotted the couple. With a smile on his face, he said, "Hope you got a good night's rest and everything was fine."

Both the man and the woman thanked the clerk for his kindness. After exchanging a few words, the elderly man changed the subject. "Young man," he said, "you're too fine a hotel man to stay in a hotel like this. How would you like for me to build a large, expensive luxury hotel in the city of New York and make you the manager of it?" Well, the young man sat there for a moment. He did not know exactly what to say. He wondered if the gentleman's mind was right. Finally, after searching for something to say, he stammered out these words: "It sounds wonderful!"

You know, that young man didn't have to put those people up for the night. He could have turned them away. He had a good reason, and people have been turned away before. Remember Bethlehem? Already every major hotel in Philadelphia had turned them away, but this young man had something about him that refused to turn them away. He wanted to help, to be kind. Do unto others. He did that. He followed the carpenter's command.

It wasn't long after that that a new hotel went up in New York City. It was one of the greatest hotels ever built. They named it the Waldorf Astoria. And the young night clerk became the manager and one of the world's greatest hotel men. The gentleman he shared his room with? Who is William Waldorf Astor.

Dr. A.J. Cronin

Dr. A.J. Cronin was a physician in England until his health broke. Unable to carry on his medical work, Dr. Cronin turned to writing. It was one of the best things that ever happened to the world of literature. For through his writings, Dr. Cronin continued his work of healing.

Dr. Cronin had an experience happen to him prior to his retirement from the medical profession. It's an experience that Dr. Cronin told that needs to be retold often. It's the story of a young nurse who was put in charge of a little boy brought into the hospital, suffering from diphtheria. The child's throat was choked with membrane, and he was given only a slight chance to live. A tube was inserted into the boy's throat to help him breathe. It was the young nurse's job to systematically clean the tube so that it would not become blocked, thereby cutting off the boy's breathing. As the young nurse sat beside the boy, tired and sleepy, she accidentally dozed off. She awakened to find the tube had become blocked.

Instead of following her instructions, the nurse bolted in panic. Hysterically, she called the doctor out of his sleep. But by the time the doctor got to the young boy, he was dead. Dr. Cronin was angry beyond expression that a child should die so needlessly by such blundering, inexcusable negligence. Of course, the nurse's career was through. She didn't deserve another chance. That night, Dr. Cronin went into his office, dipped his pen in ink, and wrote his recommendation to the board demanding her immediate expulsion. He called her in and read it with a voice trembling with resentment and anger. She stood there in pitiful silence. A tall, thin, gawky, Welsh girl. She nearly fainted with shame and remorse. "Well, have you nothing to say for yourself?" asked Dr. Cronin in a harsh voice. There was more silence, and then came a stammering plea. "Give me, uh, give me another chance."

Well, Dr. Cronin was shocked. Certainly, he had no thought of doing that. She'd made a mistake, an unforgivable mistake. There was nothing to do but punish her. He ordered her to leave the room, sealed his report, left it on his desk, and went to bed. But that night he could not sleep. He kept hearing some words from the dark distance. The words came easing from the stillness of the night. *Forgive us our trespasses.*

How often that word comes to us and how much we need forgiveness. How many times we make mistakes, unforgivable mistakes, and we need another chance. Consider the plight of the world if there was no source of forgiveness, no cross, no Christ. The next morning, Dr. Cronin went to his desk and tore up the report. In the years that followed, he watched as this slim, nervous girl became the head of a large hospital and one of the most honored nurses in all England.

Forgiveness. It's a grand word. Practice it. Practice it often.

Before It's Too Late

Thomas Carlyle lived from 1795 until 1881. He was a Scottish essayist and historian. During his lifetime, he became one of the world's greatest writers. But he was a human, and humans make mistakes.

On October 17, 1826, Carlyle married his secretary, Jane Welch. She was an intelligent, attractive, and somewhat temperamental daughter of a well-to-do doctor. Now, they had their quarrels and misunderstandings but still loved each other dearly. After their marriage, Jane continued to serve as his secretary. After several years of marriage, Jane became ill. Being a hard worker, Carlyle became so absorbed in his writings that he let Jane continue working for several weeks after she became sick. She had cancer, and it was one of the slow-growing kind. Finally, she became confined to her bed. Although Carlyle loved her dearly, he very seldom found time to stay with her very long. He was busy with his work.

When Jane died, they carried her to the cemetery for the service. It was a miserable day. It was raining hard, and the mud was deep. Following the funeral, Carlyle went back to his home. He was taking it pretty hard. He went up the stairs to Jane's room and sat down in the chair next to her bed. He sat there thinking about how little time he had spent with her and wishing so much that he had a chance to do it again. Noticing her diary on a table beside the bed, he picked it up and began to read. Suddenly, he seemed shocked. He saw it.

There on one page, she had written a single line. *Yesterday, he spent an hour with me, and it was like heaven. I love him so.*

Something dawned on him that he had not noticed before. He'd been too busy to notice that he'd meant so much to her. He thought of all the times he had gone about his work without thinking about and noticing her. Then Carlyle turned the page in the diary. There he noticed written some words that broke his heart. *I have listened all day to hear his steps in the hall,* she wrote, *but now it's late, and I guess he won't come today.*

Carlyle read a little more in the book. Then he threw it down and ran out of the house. Some of his friends found him at the grave. His face buried in the mud. His eyes were red from weeping. Tears continued to roll down his cheeks. He kept repeating over and over again: "If I had only known, if I had only known." But it was too late for Carlyle. Jane was dead.

After Jane's death, Carlyle made little attempt to write again. A historian said that he lived another 15 years weary, bored, and a partial recluse.

I tell the story with the hope that you will not make the same mistake. While our loved ones must have the money we make to live, it is the love we have that they really want. Give it now before it's too late.

Reaping the Harvest We Have Sown

Wilson Thomas Turner was sitting at the bar. The date? September 12, 1964. The place was Bradenton, Florida. *One more little drink won't hurt anything*, he thought. Turner took one more little drink. Maybe it was one for the road. Then he ordered another bottle to take home. *It's always good to have a bottle around the house, isn't it?* Turner got up from his seat, turned, and walked through the door. He got into his automobile to drive home. He had done it before. Like most folks, he thought a little toddy wouldn't affect his driving. *Some folks, you know, do their best driving with a shot or two under their belts.* He opened the door and sat down behind the steering wheel. Then he headed down the road toward home.

Turner had had a hard day. He was looking forward to seeing his son, Randall. Randall was in the fifth grade now. He'd grown up so fast. Turner was proud of his son. He always liked to spend some time with him. The automobile roared down the street. The speedometer went higher and higher. Turner didn't notice the speedometer. Maybe like a lot of other folks who drive after a shot or two, he was an expert driver. Suddenly, from out of nowhere, came a kid riding a bicycle. Turner turned, applied the brakes. He waited for a split second. Then he heard a loud thump. He looked back. The kid was on the pavement. He sped away.

Witnesses at the scene identified the car. Officers found

it later at the home of Turner. The blood was still on it. They found Turner in the attic, a bottle in his hand. It was the bottle that was good to have around the house. Officers questioned him for more than an hour. Then the news came. The boy was dead. "He just went to pieces when he was told that the boy was dead," said Sheriff Ken Gross. Turner was taken to jail. He was charged with manslaughter and leaving the scene of a fatal accident.

His attorney, Jerry Hussey, carried him a Bible. He sat in the jail day after day reading the Bible. "He's sworn up and down to his wife and to me that he'll never touch another drop of liquor," said Mr. Hussey. Turner was allowed to leave the jail long enough to attend the funeral service for the boy. It was one of the hardest funerals Turner ever had to face.

The minister tried to bring comfort in such a trying hour. They carried the casket to the grave and lowered it into the earth. The life that Turner had taken so foolishly. Nothing anyone could do would ever bring the boy back. *A little drink never hurt anyone, did it?* Well, Turner couldn't say that now because it had hurt. So awfully hard, it hurt. If there was only another chance, but it's too late now. Too late.

The story is true. It was carried by the news service. Oh, there's one other item in the story. The boy that Turner killed was Randall Turner, his 12-year-old son.

True Beauty

Ours is a youth-oriented age. We stress youth as beauty and strength – two of the things we covet the most. A tremendous amount of our time and effort and money is directed toward the adults of tomorrow. And that, in itself, isn't all wrong. For we should take stock in our youth, help them to make this a better world than it is, give them chances we never had. The only trouble is that we've done so too often at the expense of the older person.

Perhaps the most neglected person in our society is the elderly person. Too often there seems to be no room, no place for those who are in their golden years. In our quest for beauty, we've looked upon only the outside, and this has caused us to turn to youth, for it's true that they are physically prettier than the elderly. But beauty, real beauty, is to be found on the inside.

And here, many of our older adults put Hollywood's beauties to shame. Perhaps the most beautiful sight in the world is an elderly mother sitting and thinking about the time when her children were young. She cared for her children, worked like a slave for them, gave up many things she wanted in order that her children could have something. We too often forget the many meals she fixed us; how many nights she lay awake while we were sick; how many new dresses she would do without, so we could have some new clothes.

Then, too, an elderly gentleman is perhaps our best illustration of a real man. The magazines, you know, say that you have to be young and muscular to be a real man, but that's only superficial. For real manhood belongs to the man with a walking cane who's given his life working for his family, friends, and community. But now that he has slowed, now that his strength is weakened, now that his hair is gray, we forget about him and his outstanding deeds.

All of us, without exception, are indebted to the elderly. Few of us could began to match the real beauty and strength that is theirs. They have worked and worried, slaved and sacrificed that our world would be a better one for us. Now they are often neglected, unwanted, forgotten. I guess more than anything else in the whole world, an elderly person just wants to be appreciated instead of ignored. It appears that it's not asking too much for youth to give up a few hours, a few wishes, a few dollars to say to the elderly, "You're still loved, wanted, and appreciated. We have not [forgotten], nor will we forget your great love and sacrifice for us."

The Creator, in his wisdom, saw fit to reserve real beauty and real strength until our golden years. What we call beauty and strength in our younger years is but a fainting, fading, passing resemblance of the real thing. It takes years upon years to develop those traits. Why should we hesitate to sacrifice so little for those who have given so much?

Honesty Is the Best Policy

Some time ago, in Brentwood, New York, Mrs. Raymond Bates found her two youngest children, Deborah and Andrew, eating tranquilizer pills. Knowing the seriousness of the issue, she immediately asked their older brother, Timothy, if he had eaten any of the pills. He said that he had not. Mrs. Bates rushed the children to the hospital, and Deborah, age 2, and Andrew, 4, both had their stomachs pumped. Timothy, denying that he had eaten any of the pills, did not have his stomach pumped. It was a crucial situation for Mrs. Bates, for the pills that the children had eaten could have very easily killed them. It was of utmost importance that she be told the truth by her children. To have lied in a situation like that could have meant death for any of them.

You know, there are many situations like that in life. Several times, our physical life depends on whether or not we're willing to tell the truth, face the facts. Failure to do so will often mean death or serious injury. But deeper than this is the fact that we must be willing to tell the truth about our intangible being also. And here's where most of us are willing to try to get by on a half-truth, sometimes even a flat lie. We haven't been honest with ourselves here. We've told ourselves that everything is OK, it'll work out all right. So we've gone on ignoring our inner being, pretending that there will be a time to take care of that. We've even built up a conception that there's a great Santa Claus in the sky who will bring us everything we need at the right time. We've lied to ourselves in telling ourselves that we have no obligation any higher than ourselves. We have fooled ourselves into thinking that if there is life after death, everybody will enjoy it equally and not just a pious few.

When I break a bone and it needs setting, I don't dare fool myself into thinking that it would be all right if I left it alone, and everything will work out OK by itself.

If I have cancer, I don't go around telling people that there's a great fairyland cancer doctor who will cure me. When I had my heart attack, I didn't ask for a knife that I could operate on myself. No. In all of these things I told myself, and I tell myself, the truth: that I need help from beyond myself, from someone whose business it is to help in those situations. To do less in the spiritual realm would be equally as foolish.

Don't make the mistake with your spiritual life that Timothy Bates made with his physical life. When Mrs. Bates went to check on the children the next morning, Deborah and Andrew, who had their stomachs pumped were fine. Timothy, age 8, was dead.

Honesty is the best policy ... in all matters.

Jealousy Destroys

Sir Christopher Wren, the builder of St. Paul's Cathedral in London, was a famous architect of the 17th and 18th centuries. Once he was building a church building in London when he was severely criticized by a group of jealous architects. He was told that his type of architecture would not support the massive roof he was putting on the building. After much debate and Sir Christopher's insistence that his architecture would easily support the roof, the officials ordered Sir Christopher to put in additional supporting pillars. Sir Christopher, reluctantly and insisting that they were not needed, did as he was ordered. Here was the story of a genius in his field who was forced to go against his own conclusions because of the envy of his competitors.

Funny sometimes the way jealousy gets into our system. Someone can do something just a little better than we can. Someone gets recognized as being just a little more capable than we are. Someone rises above us, and we seek to pull them down. It seems that if Sir Christopher had found a new way to support a roof that his competitors would rejoice with him and learn from him. But such wasn't the case. They turned against him. Scorned and laughed and ridiculed him. And sold the public a bill of goods that his way just wouldn't work.

There are many cases like that in history. Someone comes along with something new, different, better, and we unloose our jealousy on it. We are so self-centered that we will not allow ourselves to recognize greatness when it comes. Rather than paying tribute to greatness, we attempt, and often succeed, in pulling the other person down.

Galileo knew something about this, and they treated the fisher of men in that way, you know. He came with a new way, a more excellent method, a clearer revelation of what God was like, and his fellow counterparts sought a way to destroy him. He won the hearts of a few men, but men in his profession turned against him. He was doing something new, something that he knew would work. He had full confidence in himself and in his work. But jealousy burned in the hearts of the recognized religious leaders. They sought to destroy him. Rather than listen to what this man had to say and see if it was true or not, they closed their ears and would not hear his message. And, prompted by jealousy and selfishness, set about to get rid of him. He was a threat to their position.

Let someone get in front of us, and rather than joining them, we try to pull them down. But life never lets anyone climb higher by pulling another down.

Well, 50 years after Sir Christopher had finished the church building, some painters were doing some repair work on the church. It was then discovered that the additional pillars that Sir Christopher placed in the building missed the roof by two feet.

Greatness cannot be destroyed by jealousy. Greatness is always at least two feet taller.

Not Unlike Peter

"Then seizing him, they led him away and took him into the house of the high priest. Peter followed at a distance. And when some there had kindled a fire in the middle of the courtyard and had sat down together, Peter sat down with them" (Luke 22:54-55).

After Jesus was arrested in the garden of Gethsemane, he was carried to the house of Joseph Caiaphas. Caiaphas was the high priest that year, although it was his father-in-law, Annas, who had the real power. In all probability, the party walked up a flight of steps in the southern part of Jerusalem to reach the house of Caiaphas. Some steps have been excavated, which led to the spot where many believe the house of Caiaphas stood. It is possible to walk those very steps today.

The Church of St. Peter in Gallicantu, which means *cockcrow*, is a lovely little church building constructed by the Augustinian fathers on the site where they accept as that of the house of Caiaphas. The church gets its name from the fact that Peter denied he knew Jesus three times in the courtyard before the 3 a.m. hour – the time of the cockcrow. In the life of Jesus, we have some hours between 3 o'clock in the morning and about 6 o'clock in the morning during which we don't know what happened to him.

A visitor to the Church of St. Peter in Gallicantu today will be taken down into the basement to examine a pit carved from the rock. The pit is very small and has only one opening large enough for a person to enter it. The opening is at the top of the pit. The pit was part of the jail located there. Perhaps Jesus, being tried and condemned by an illegal makeshift Sanhedrin, meeting in the early hours, was brought to this pit to spend the next few hours. In the 88th Psalm, one can read what could have been the feelings of Jesus, if indeed he was lowered into this pit.

Peter denied his Lord that night. He did so, I feel, not so much from cowardice as from bewilderment and confusion. He did not know what Jesus expected him to do. Did he not get rebuked by the Lord in the garden of Gethsemane just a short time before when he fought for the safety and release of Jesus?

Certainly, Peter was confused as to what course of action to follow. Standing on the balcony of the Church of St. Peter in Gallicantu, you can see where the courtyard was that Peter denied his Lord. And as you gaze in that direction, you aren't quite as fast to point the accusing finger at the big fisherman. You can recall those times when you too denied the Lord by silence or inaction. It is one thing to find fault and blame. It is another thing, altogether, to take a very deep look into one's own commitment. We aren't nearly as perfect as we sometimes think we are.

As you leave this beautiful little church building, you do so thinking that you need to spend more time on the log in your own eye and less on the splinter in your neighbor's eye. Jesus was speaking to each of us when he gave that advice.

Christ's Journey to the Cross

"And when they had mocked him, they took off the purple robe and put his own clothes on him. Then they led him out to crucify him" (Mark 15:20).

Calvary was located outside the city walls of Jerusalem. Crucifixions inside the walls were forbidden. So the Romans, who alone could order the death penalty, made sure that crucifixions were executed where the general public could get a good view. This was an effective reminder for any of those Jews who had ideas concerning opposition to Roman authority.

We are told that Christ was scourged before he was crucified. Scourging consisted of a lashing with leather thongs tipped on the end with metal. The prisoner was stripped of his clothing. He was bent over, and he was whipped on the naked flesh on his back. The result was sometimes fatal to the prisoner. Certainly, following his scourging, Jesus was very weak. He was bruised and beaten. His body was bloody. The Romans showed little mercy to prisoners. So Christ was forced to carry the cross on which he was to be crucified to Calvary, the place of the skull. Whether the spot got its name from its appearance resembling a skull or from skulls left from previous crucifixions, we aren't sure. What we are sure of is that Calvary was the place of death.

On his way to Calvary, weak from the scourging, Christ fell under the weight of his cross. It was so heavy, and he was so weak, he had to have help. Christ was dependent upon his fellow man, just as we are. It was Simon, the Cyrenian, who carried the cross for Christ. Simon eased the load and lightened the burden of the one who had eased the loads and lightened the burdens of so many. Since Cyrene was a city in [present-day] Libya in northern Africa, there's a good possibility that Simon was a black person. Whether he was or wasn't, isn't important. What is important is that he carried the cross of Christ. He helped a brother who needed help.

Perhaps one of the two traditional sites we have today called Calvary is the authentic one. Or perhaps we will never know where Calvary is physically. Does it matter? Calvary can be anywhere. Calvary can be everywhere. Whenever we die to self and come alive to God and our fellow human beings, there is Calvary. Wherever we lay down our lives and stretch out our selfish hands to our fellow human beings, there will be our Calvary.

This Jesus we worship wasn't spared the pain and hurt of life. He was no Buddha protected from the old, diseased, and miserable. No, no. Our Christ knew suffering and hurt. He had seen it in the eyes of the mother whose daughter he was requested to heal. He had seen it in the humility of the Roman officer whose slave was sick. He tasted it in the death of Lazarus, and he cried with Mary and Martha in their sorrow. Now, he personally was the sufferer. Pain racked his body; hurt broke his heart.

The crucifixion of Christ did not stop on that Judean hillside 2,000 years ago. Not a day has passed when he has not been crucified again. So many times, in so many ways, we drive the spikes of selfishness into his hands. Christ died for me – those four words have changed the lives of countless individuals. Their full impact upon the world will never be realized. And it was at Calvary that Christ died. We must face Calvary too if we are to live with him.

Our Own Mount of Olives

"Those who went ahead and those who followed shouted, 'Hosanna! Blessed is he who comes in the name of the Lord! Blessed is the coming kingdom of our father David! Hosanna in the highest heaven!'" (Mark 11:9-10).

To the east of Jerusalem, across the Kidron Valley, a little more than half a mile – a Sabbath day's journey – is the Mount of Olives. From its summit, one can see the panorama of Jerusalem. Some 15 miles to the east is the Dead Sea. Many are the memories associated with this holy hill. It was from the Mount of Olives Jesus looked over Jerusalem and wept. A chapel is built on the traditional site of his weeping. It is called Dominus Flevit, which is Latin for *the Lord wept*. Twice in the life of Jesus, we know he wept – at the death of his friend Lazarus and when he looked over the city of Jerusalem from the Mount of Olives. No doubt Jesus came often to this beautiful mount at evening when other men would go to their homes. Here amid the grove of olive trees, he would rest. Here in the stillness of the night, he could pray to the Father without interruption. Perhaps it was, as tradition says, on this hillside that he taught his disciples to pray what we call the Lord's Prayer. The Church of the Pater Noster, that is "our Father," is built on the traditional site. Its walls contain the Lord's Prayer in more than 65 different languages. Truly the prayer has been uttered in many times that number of languages.

Located on the top of the Mount of Olives was the village of Bethphage. Here his disciples found the donkey he rode into Jerusalem on Palm Sunday. The town was a probable dwelling place of Galileans, and Jesus would have been among familiar people. The Galileans were scorned by the more pious and religious citizens of Judea and Jerusalem.

Down the mountainside, Jesus rode that day. People along the way paved the road with palm branches and called him king. Both sides of the dusty road were lined with spectators singing praises to him. Little did they realize, that in five days, this man who rode the donkey as a symbol of peace would be crucified by the Roman government as a revolutionary and troublemaker.

What thoughts were in his mind as he rode past the garden of Gethsemane? Were tears still flowing as he crossed the Kidron Valley and entered Jerusalem through the Golden Gate? And as he entered the temple area, did he think of turning back? Following his crucifixion and resurrection, Jesus would come back to the Mount of Olives. He would walk through its groves and remember all that had taken place on its slopes. And here on this mountainside, he would be lifted up into heaven. Some 500 years later, some devout followers of his would erect the Chapel of the Ascension in memory of that magnificent event. It is a bit of irony, or perhaps the plan of Providence, that on the Mount of Olives, Jesus faced his darkest night in the garden of Gethsemane and his brightest day at the site of the ascension.

The Mount of Olives reminds one of many things concerning our Lord. It was a kind of refuge away from the crowd for him. It was a place where he could be alone with his Father. We need a place like that also. It was a place of sorrow, and each of us must face that side of life. But it was also the site of his ascension, where he went to be at home with his Father. Hopefully, each of us will have our own Mount of Olives.

The Bethany Perspective

"Six days before the Passover, Jesus came to Bethany, where Lazarus lived, whom Jesus had raised from the dead. Here a dinner was given in Jesus' honor. Martha served, while Lazarus was among those reclining at the table with him" (John 12:1-2).

Bethany lies on the southeastern slope of the Mount of Olives, nearly two miles east of Jerusalem. It was the hometown of three very close friends of Jesus – Mary, Martha, and Lazarus. While Jerusalem gives us its view of the personality of Jesus, Bethany presents its view also. It was in this little community that Jesus came to rest when he visited Jerusalem. Following the Palm Sunday events, he brought his disciples to Bethany to spend the night. Here, away from the crowds, he could rest and fellowship with a small group of friends. It was in Bethany that Simon the leper invited Jesus to a meal. While they were eating, Mary broke a very expensive jar of perfume and poured it on the head of Jesus. The perfume could have been sold for more than $300, nearly a year's wages. It was with reckless devotion that Mary loved her Lord.

Once, Jesus was sitting and teaching in the home of Lazarus. They had just finished a meal, and Martha was busy cleaning the table and washing the dishes. Mary, who should have been helping Martha, had become so enraptured with the words of Christ that she forgot her duties. Martha entreated Jesus to remind Mary of her duties, but the gentle Galilean instead reminded Martha that the dishes could wait while the words of life were being spoken.

Jesus was a man of deep compassion, and when told by Mary that her brother Lazarus had died, he wept from sorrow. Being shown the place where Lazarus had been buried, Jesus called him out from the grave and death. This act, incidentally, hastened the death of Jesus by the religious authorities. It was at the graveside of Lazarus that Jesus uttered words, which today are spoken at nearly every Christian funeral. Speaking to a deeply grieved Martha, Jesus reminded her of his life-giving mission. "Jesus said to her, 'I am the resurrection and the life. The one who believes in me will live, even though they die; and whoever lives by believing in me will never die ...'" (John 11:25-26).

There is in modern Bethany, a church building built on the traditional site of the home of Lazarus. It is called the Church of [Saint] Lazarus. On its walls are inscribed those words of Jesus. If you visit Bethany today, you will be shown a tomb behind the Church of Lazarus. Here, supposedly, Lazarus was laid only to rise again through the love of Christ. It's a typical tomb cut out of the rock and containing a burial chamber in which the dead lay on a slab of rock.

You know, life makes demands upon us, both public and private. We are called upon to express our faith to the masses and also to our friends. It is with us, as it was with Christ, that we gain strength from our private circle of friends to face the public masses. Whenever we are exhausted from our public duties, we can retire to our small circle of intimate friends for renewed strength, and that is what Christ did often at Bethany.

The Jordan

"At that time Jesus came from Nazareth in Galilee and was baptized by John in the Jordan" (Mark 1:9).

Probably the most famous river in the world is the Jordan River. It isn't a large stream. In fact, many people would hesitate to even call it a river at all. It begins near Banias in the area where Caesarea Philippi stood in New Testament times and flows the distance of approximately 100 miles to the Dead Sea.

It is a very crooked and weaving stream between the Sea of Galilee and the Dead Sea, the two major bodies of water which it connects. The river covers a distance of nearly 200 miles in that 65-mile stretch. The river is from 3 to 10 feet deep and has an average width of between 90 and 100 feet. It contains some 30 species of fish, the most famous being known as St. Peter's fish. According to tradition, it was in the mouth of this species that the famous disciple found the coin.

The river begins at a height of some 1,200 feet above sea level. It ends at a depth of some 1,300 feet below sea level. Most of the stream is below the level of the sea. This causes the temperatures along its course to rise as high as 118 degrees in places during the month of August.

The prophet Elisha sent the Syrian army general Naaman to the Jordan to be healed of his leprosy. Naaman reluctantly washed himself in the water and was healed. And it was over this river that Moses looked into the Promised Land from

Mount Nebo. John the Baptist centered much of his ministry around the river. He used its water to baptize his converts. Jesus was baptized in the Jordan by John the Baptist. John was very reluctant to baptize Jesus and only did so upon the insistence of the Galilean. The traditional site of the baptism of Jesus is about four miles north of the Dead Sea.

The Jordan represents a dividing line to biblical students. It was over this river that Joshua led the Israelites. It divided the wandering Israelites from their past meanderings and their new home in Canaan. It also is a dividing line in the life of Christ. For it was at the Jordan that he publicly embarked upon his ministry. Perhaps, as legend has it, Jesus was baptized at the same crossing used by the children of Israel to enter the Promised Land.

Today, literally thousands of Christians visit the river to be baptized and to renew their baptism as a symbol of their faith. Pilgrims even take home water from this stream with which to baptize in their own land. Millions of Christians who have never seen the Jordan have symbolically crossed it. For they too have crossed over that dividing line in making public their ministry for this carpenter from Nazareth, regardless of the occupation they fulfill.

We said that the Jordan was probably the most famous river in the world. And that fame is due primarily to its association with the man from Galilee.

The Wilderness

"At once the Spirit sent him out into the wilderness, and he was in the wilderness forty days, being tempted by Satan. He was with the wild animals, and angels attended him" (Mark 1:12-13).

The wilderness spoken of in the temptation experience of Jesus is unlike the conception most Americans have of a wilderness. When the word *wilderness* is spoken, we usually associate it with a region of tremendous undergrowth and trees. The wilderness which Jesus faced was one of rolling hills, nearly barren of any growth. Tradition places the area where Jesus spent his 40 days in the wilderness as being between Jerusalem and the Dead Sea. It's an almost treeless area of scant vegetation except during the rainy season when grass grows. The area is some 15 miles wide and 35 miles long. A visitor to the Holy Land today can see to the north of Jericho the traditional Mount of Temptation. Supposedly, this is the mountain spoken of in the wilderness experience.

The temptation of Jesus followed immediately on the heels of his baptism. We are told that he was led by the Holy Spirit into the desert. Christ had made a public confession of his faith in God. Now that faith was to be tested. Christ needed to know before he set out on the journey if he had the requirements to finish the journey. He was to later remind his followers: "Suppose one of you wants to build a tower. Won't you first sit down and estimate the cost to see if you have enough money to complete it?" (Luke 14:28).

It was lonely in the wilderness. Jesus went in alone. He knew that the time would come when he would have to make important decisions alone. He had to prepare himself for that time. We are told that for 40 days he fought the struggle with his tempter. He had no other to help him in his struggle there in that wilderness except for the presence of God.

During these days, Jesus went without food. It was while he was extremely hungry that he was tempted to use his power to turn stones into bread, but Christ refused. It was the beginning of a pattern to be used throughout the whole of his public ministry. He would never use his power in a selfish manner. This pattern reached its pinnacle at the cross when he refused to excuse himself from the suffering and dying.

It was in the wilderness that Jesus fought his greatest battle. It was here that he first set his face toward Jerusalem. It was here, alone and hungry, that Jesus conquered his supreme test. He did not break. He did not bend. He had been called to a high and holy task. He met and defeated his tempter. Now he was prepared to go back into the world.

There is a wilderness experience for each of us. There is a time when [we are] faced with which road of life to follow. We fight the struggle within the depths of our very own heart. Other battles will follow, but the major battle of our life is out in the wilderness when we are alone and hungry. The temptations we face, like those of Christ, are always extremely attractive. The wilderness is a very ugly and desolate place, and the temptations are extremely tempting. Few win out over the temptations of the wilderness, but those who do can walk toward Jerusalem and a waiting cross. For their life belongs to God, and it is his power which sustains them.

The Jericho Perspective

"Then they came to Jericho. As Jesus and his disciples, together with a large crowd, were leaving the city, a blind man, Bartimaeus (which means 'son of Timaeus'), was sitting by the roadside begging" (Mark 10:46).

Jericho was a two-day journey from Jerusalem in the time of Jesus. Today, the distance of about 15 miles can be covered in about 30 minutes. The city is located about five miles north of the Dead Sea. Since the city is more than 800 feet below sea level, it is extremely hot in the summer but ideal in the winter. The oldest known evidence of civilization in the world is at Jericho. Archaeologists have found remains from a civilization dating back to before 7000 B.C. Here, perhaps man first learned to live together as an organized group.

Not far from Jericho is the place in the Jordan River where tradition says Jesus was baptized by John. Immediately to the north of Jericho, one can see the Mount of Temptation. Supposedly, it was on that mount where Jesus was shown all the kingdoms of the world. Of course, the kingdoms were shown in the mind of Jesus as it is impossible to see all the world from any mountain.

Nevertheless, one can still see Mount Hermon, one of the original sources of the Jordan River, about a hundred miles to the north, if the weather is clear. To the southwest of Jericho, one can see the area of the wilderness where Christ was tested. In this wilderness, Jesus was tempted to turn the stones into bread. The implication was that if Jesus would give people bread, they would follow him. Politicians have long believed that. The next temptation was that of serving his tempter in return for power over the world. He was promised the bounty of the world if he would only yield to the tempter. Finally, he was tempted to jump from the highest point of the temple in Jerusalem. Here the implication was to use magic to fool the masses. All the temptations, Christ refused.

It was in Jericho that little Zacchaeus climbed the sycamore tree and made it immortal. He wanted to see this man among men. To his complete amazement, Christ commanded that he come down from the tree and take him home as a guest. The words of Jesus so captivated this little Jewish tax collector, hated by his fellow Jews, that he was willing to give the poor half of the money he had spent his lifetime acquiring. And to think that some are offended when urged to give a tithe! A sycamore tree still stands in the heart of Jericho today, symbolic of that transforming event.

Here, also, is where blind Bartimaeus came to Christ. As he called out the name of Jesus from the roadside, the crowds sought to hush his pleas. They scolded him and told him to be quiet. But this was his chance to meet the Master, to see again and live again, and an army could not have hushed his pleas. When he came to Jesus, his eyes were opened, and he was given his sight. Scripture says he did a normal thing following the regaining of his sight; he followed Jesus.

Jericho was the winter home of King Herod the Great. It was here that Herod died probably in 4 B.C. Shortly before his death, Herod ordered some of the prominent citizens of the town to be killed so that there would be tears shed at the time of his death.

In Jericho, Jesus ministered to his fellow man. Hopefully, we can all find our Jericho each time our life crosses the path of another.

The Two Seas

"Jesus left there and went along the Sea of Galilee. Then he went up on a mountainside and sat down" (Matthew 15:29).

The lowest spot in the world is the Dead Sea in the Holy Land. It is nearly 1,300 feet below sea level. The Dead Sea contains approximately 25% salt as compared to about 5% of salt content for the oceans. The Dead Sea is supplied by the Jordan River and a few small seasonal streams. When I first tasted the water in the Dead Sea, it sent a terrible taste through my body, despite the fact that I had only touched my tongue with a couple of drops of water. The water on my hands soon dried, and I was forced to take soap and fresh water before I could remove the feeling which the dried Dead Sea water left.

Just a few miles up from the Dead Sea is the Sea of Galilee. It is one of the most beautiful small bodies of water in the world. The Sea of Galilee is about 13 miles long and 8 miles wide and is some 680 feet below sea level. Its greatest step is about 200 feet. There's no salt in the water of the Sea of Galilee. It is fresh water. Around the Dead Sea, hardly anything grows, but around the Sea of Galilee is one of the most fertile valleys in the world. The Jordan River is also the major source of water for the Sea of Galilee. The big difference in the two seas is that the Sea of Galilee takes water in and gives water out while the Dead Sea only takes water in with no outlet. The only way water can get out of the Dead Sea is for it to be taken out through evaporation.

You know, there's a symbol of life in these two seas. The Dead Sea is exactly that – dead. It takes all the water in but gives no water out. The Sea of Galilee takes water in and gives water out. The Sea of Galilee is surrounded by a living, growing beautiful valley. The Dead Sea is surrounded by naked wilderness. And so it is with life. The person who knows how to give as well as receive will find life to be beautiful. The person who knows only how to receive and not how to give will find life to be only a barren wilderness.

One of the basic fundamentals of life is that we learn how to give. If we never learn this, then we never really learn to live in a true sense of the word. I have known people who only take, who hoard everything they get, who aren't interested in anyone but themselves. And, on the other hand, I've also known people who know how to share what life passes on to them. I think you know the difference.

I don't particularly like to visit the Dead Sea, but I love very much to stand on the Mount of Beatitudes and look over the beautiful Sea of Galilee. So it is with people. Those who only get and never give are never pleasant to be around. A person is thankful when he leaves their presence. But a person who can get and give finds he has people who truly love and appreciate his company.

Oh, there's one other thing about the Dead Sea which I remember. It doesn't smell very good either. Perhaps there's a symbolism there also, but I'll let you figure it out.

The Samaritan Woman

"So he came to a town in Samaria called Sychar, near the plot of ground Jacob had given to his son Joseph. Jacob's Well was there, and Jesus, tired as he was from the journey, sat down by the well. It was about noon" (John 4:5-6).

Palestine in the time of Jesus was divided into three sections: In the South was Judea, the region where Christ was born. In the North was Galilee, the region where Christ grew up. In between Judea and Galilee was Samaria. The Scriptures tell us of a journey Jesus took through Samaria. It also reminds us that Jews did not normally travel through Samaria. In fact, the Jews considered the Samaritans such a low-class people that no self-respecting Jew had any dealing whatsoever with a Samaritan.

We know that Jesus and his disciples stopped at Jacob's Well in Samaria to rest and eat. The disciples left Jesus at the well and went into Sychar to get some food. It was about noon, and Jesus was resting at the well, waiting for the return of his disciples. As he waited, a Samaritan woman came to the well to draw water. To the casual reader, there's nothing unusual about this, but to one who is familiar with the customs of the day, the oddity is immediately recognized. No woman ever drew water in the middle of the day. Only work absolutely necessary was performed while the heat was so intense. Women drew their water at the close of the day when temperatures were much cooler. It was a social event for the village women, and as they drew water, they could catch up on the latest gossip. Evidently, the respectable women had so ignored, excluded, and embarrassed this woman that she came to draw water at a time when she would be sure no one else would be present.

Then Jesus did a very unusual thing. He spoke to this Samaritan woman. He asked her for a drink, and the request opened up a conversation which was to change her life. She replied to his request by reminding him of the racial prejudice between the Jews and Samaritans, but then Christ lifted her vision to a higher plane by offering her living water. When she again injected the race issue into the conversation by mentioning the Samaritan temple on Mount Gerizim, located to the south and visible from Jacob's Well, Christ reminded her that the place where one worshiped was unimportant. The important part of worship was the how – in spirit and truth.

It is of supreme importance that Christ first revealed his identity to this woman of the world – married five times and living with a sixth man. To the Jew, this woman was as low a human as one could be. It is significant that John included this story in his gospel. None of the other gospels contain it. Here is Christ revealing, for the first time, his messiahship to a sinful Samaritan woman. In effect, John is saying that God's love reaches to the very lowest and least of all people. The love of God knows absolutely no limits.

You can still drink from Jacob's Well today. Each time I stop there, I pause to drink from the very deep stream. For centuries and centuries, the well has been giving life. But each time I drink, I'm reminded of the living water which Christ gave to that Samaritan woman. And, like he said, this living water is available to us no matter who we are or where we worship. Indeed, God's love knows no limits.

The Nazareth Perspective

"And he went and lived in a town called Nazareth. So was fulfilled what was said through the prophets, that he would be called a Nazarene" (Matthew 2:23).

Nazareth isn't mentioned in the Old Testament. We infer from this that not much importance was given to the town. In fact, we are led to believe that the town was even scorned by many, for was it not Nathanael who asked, "Nazareth! Can anything good come from there?" (John 1:46).

The town was not located on any of the main thoroughfares. It lies slightly back out of the mainstream of traffic. The city owes its importance, of course, to the fact that it was the home of the Galilean carpenter. In a very real way, he put the town on the map. Mention of the town is made some 28 times in the New Testament, and each time it is in connection with Jesus.

The town lies in a valley surrounded by hills, which rise like amphitheaters. It is located in lower Galilee. Thus, the one who came from Nazareth has often been known simply as the Galilean. The little city is located about 80 miles to the north of Jerusalem. To the west is the beautiful Mediterranean Sea, approximately 20 miles away. To the northeast is the breathtaking Sea of Galilee.

There's a spring in Nazareth which never runs dry. In the days when Christ was a boy, it was the only source of water in the city. His mother, Mary, must have come often to the spring to fill her jars, stopping a while to socialize with the other ladies drawing water. Many times, perhaps, Christ himself drank from the refreshing stream. It still flows to this day, and today it's known as Mary's Well.

The area around Nazareth is rocky and rather rough. In the lovely Plain of Esdraelon, located just to the south of the city, was an international highway in the days of Jesus. It was called the Via Maris, or the "Way of the Sea" or the "Road of the Sea," and it linked Damascus with Gaza and Egypt. To the east, one can see Mount Tabor, a possible site of the transfiguration. To the west, one can see Mount Carmel and remember the struggle that Elijah had there with the prophets of Baal.

Jesus wasn't very popular in Nazareth after he began his public ministry. In fact, following one sermon in the synagogue, he was literally run out of town. The townspeople intended to push Jesus down a hillside and then stone him, but he was able to walk through their ranks and out of the city. The Hill of Precipitation, commemorating the event, is shown to visitors of Nazareth today. Some people blame their place of birth or their natural surroundings for their shortcomings, but not that man. Nazareth may have been a backward town, but there was nothing backward about the man who made the town famous. His vision was forward toward eternity. No place of birth, no prejudice on the part of other people, no lack of sophistication ever hindered him from rising to the heights God had called him. The town owes whatever fame and recognition it has to the one who grew up there, tending his father's carpenter shop, and perhaps, even occasionally, keeping watch over a flock of sheep in the field.

Nazareth was the place where the Galilean lived. In that respect, hopefully there's a little of Nazareth in each of us.

The Place of the Miraculous Feeding

"Taking the five loaves and the two fish and looking up to heaven, he gave thanks and broke the loaves. Then he gave them to his disciples to distribute to the people. He also divided the two fish among them all" (Mark 6:41).

The area of Tabgha, located between Capernaum and Magdala on the western shore of the Sea of Galilee, is a very historic area. For it was here, according to tradition, where Jesus fed the 5,000 men plus additional women and children. Here also, he fed the disciples following his resurrection. Tabgha gets its name from the corruption of a Greek word, which means *seven springs*. At Tabgha, in 1932, the ruins of an ancient church were discovered. Today, another structure known as the Church of the Multiplication stands over the ruins. The floor of that ancient church, dating at least back to the fourth century, contains mosaics which are renowned throughout the world for their beauty and realism. They depict the waterbirds and flowers of the area, and symbols of the five loaves and two fish of the miracle.

This miracle of Jesus – the feeding of the 5,000 – was considered an impressive event by the early church. Incidentally, it is the only miracle mentioned in all four Gospels in the New Testament. It is John who tells us of the young boy, which Andrew brought to Christ, and how Christ used the lad's five loaves and two fish to feed the multitude. After the feeding, each disciple filled his basket with the food that was left over.

Near the Church of the Multiplication is the Church of the Primacy [of Peter]. It's located on the shore of the Sea of Galilee. It's built on the spot where tradition says Jesus is supposed to have fed Peter and the six other disciples after a night of fruitless fishing.

The structure is built over a rock, which today is known as the Table of Christ. Tradition says it is the rock used by Jesus to eat the morning meal of fish with his followers. It was here that Jesus gave to Peter the threefold repetition symbolic of a legal transfer. Feed my lambs. Tend my sheep. Feed my sheep. Jesus was giving the responsibility of his church to Peter and the others.

The Church of the Primacy is a lovely little structure. Waves from the Sea of Galilee splash beneath it. The area around it is lovely and peaceful, a probable contrast from the biblical days when this area was teaming with people and commerce.

Two great truths come out of the events which came to pass in this area. In the case of the multiplication of the loaves and fish, the truth is that little, when given to him who is the Creator, can be transformed into a lot. The young boy willing to share the lunch, which his mother packed for him, found this to be true. The other truth concerns the disciples. They discovered that Jesus can be completely trusted. Following his directions, despite having caught nothing during an entire night of fishing, they cast where he told them and caught 153 fish. We must never forget that they cast their nets in sheer faith. As one stands here in this area, his thoughts are varied, but one wish stands out. That these two great truths can perhaps come alive again in us, even today.

The Transfiguration Site

"After six days Jesus took with him Peter, James and John the brother of James, and led them up a high mountain by themselves. There he was transfigured before them. His face shone like the sun, and his clothes became as white as the light" (Matthew 17:1-2).

Two mountains in the Holy Land are revered as the Mountain of Transfiguration. Like many other sites of the Holy Land, one has to decide which site he prefers as being authentic, if indeed either is. Since the fourth century, Mount Tabor has been accepted by many as the Mount of Transfiguration. Mount Tabor is about five miles east of Nazareth and 12 miles west of the southern tip of the Sea of Galilee. Although the mountain is only 1,843 feet high, one can see a far distance from its summit. Atop Mount Tabor, you can see Mount Carmel about 25 miles to the west, on the edge of the Mediterranean Sea. You can also see Mount Hermon nearly 50 miles to the north. To the south and west of Mount Tabor is the Plain of Esdraelon, also known as the Plain of Jezreel.

The other spot which some considered to be the Mountain of Transfiguration is Mount Hermon. It's about 30 miles north of the Sea of Galilee. The highest point of this snow-capped mountain is 9,101 feet above sea level. Just south of Mount Hermon is Caesarea Philippi. The fact that Jesus was mentioned as being in this area just prior to the transfiguration experience is accepted by some as evidence of Mount

Hermon being the Mount of Transfiguration. The truth is that we don't know where the Mount of Transfiguration is, and it really doesn't matter because it was not the location which was important, but the event.

Jesus took Peter, James, and John and led them up a high mountain. Then something mysterious and exciting happened. As the disciples looked on, the face of Jesus became exceedingly bright. His clothes became as white as light. Then the three disciples recognized two men with Jesus – Moses and Elijah. Moses represented the old law through which God had sought to save man from his sinfulness. Elijah represented the prophets whom God had sent to lead the people into his kingdom. And Jesus, of course, was God's final and most perfect method of winning people to his way.

Suddenly, a shining cloud came over the group, and a voice was heard speaking from that cloud: "This is my Son, whom I love; with him I am well pleased" (Matthew 3:17). It was such a terrifying experience for the disciples that they fell on their faces. During the experience, Peter, in his excitement, wanted to build three buildings of worship on that mountain. One was to be for Jesus, one for Moses, and one for Elijah. Peter had tasted a mountaintop spiritual experience. He did not want to go back down into the valley. But Jesus would not let Peter build those houses of worship. No. Jesus took his disciples and went back down into the valley where the suffering of life was.

There was a young boy suffering from epilepsy waiting for him upon his return. You know, we all need, occasionally, our Mountain of Transfiguration experiences. But to stay on the mountain, apart from the sin and suffering of humanity, is contrary to the will of God.

The Mount of Beatitudes

"Now when Jesus saw the crowds, he went up on a mountainside and sat down. His disciples came to him, and he began to teach them" (Matthew 5:1-2).

If one wishes to locate the Mount of Beatitudes in the Holy Land, he has to accept what tradition says. For it is tradition alone which identifies the site of the most profound sermon in history. The spot is placed on the northwest shoreline of the Sea of Galilee, on a hill high above a little place called Tabgha.

"Blessed are the poor in spirit, for theirs is the kingdom of heaven" (Matthew 5:3).

For centuries, it has been accepted that Jesus began his immortal sermon on this hillside. It would seem fitting, for the view from this traditional site is absolutely beautiful. To the north is Capernaum, the adopted home of Jesus. To the south is Magdala, home of Mary Magdalene. From here, one can see the city of Tiberias built by Herod Antipas and named after the Roman emperor Tiberius. Built over a cemetery, the city was avoided by devout Jews.

"Blessed are the peacemakers, for they will be called children of God" (Matthew 5:9).

Above the beautiful Sea of Galilee, you can see the Golan Heights area. You can see the gun emplacements used by the Syrians. The contrast is bitter. "You are the salt of the earth. … You are the light of the world. A town built on a hill cannot be hidden" (Matthew 5:13-14).

You look to the north in the city of Safed. Was it this city Jesus pointed toward as he spoke? Looking down on the Sea of Galilee, you wonder how many lives those words have changed. "You have heard that it was said, 'Love your neighbor and hate your enemy.' But I tell you, love your enemies and pray for those who persecute you, that you may be children of your Father in heaven" (Matthew 5:43-45).

You close your eyes and listen. You go back across the centuries in your mind, and you imagine the scene that day. You can see the surprise spread throughout the crowd gathered here on the hillside as Jesus spoke those shocking words: "So when you give to the needy, do not announce it with trumpets, as the hypocrites do in the synagogues and on the streets, to be honored by others ..." (Matthew 6:2).

You listen and you can hear his words blowing in the wind. For a moment, you touch back into the present, wandering if indeed it was here on this side that he preached that sermon. Then suddenly it doesn't matter if it was here or over there or somewhere else. What matters is that he did preach it.

You look around this lovely area and see the variety of crops growing. You see the lilies of the field and the birds of the air. Suddenly, you realize where Jesus gathered his food for thought. It was here. All around us. Down on the Sea of Galilee, you notice a storm has begun. How quickly these waters can become rough and dangerous. You recall the incident when the disciples were frightened by a storm on these very waters and how a lowly Galilean hushed the storm.

"When Jesus had finished saying these things, the crowds were amazed at his teaching, because he taught as one who had authority, and not as their teachers of the law" (Matthew 7:28-29).

So Matthew makes his comment on the sermon. Later others were to report: "No one ever spoke the way this man does" (John 7:46). The Sermon on the Mount, perhaps preached here on the Mount of Beatitudes, has had its profound effect upon the life of mankind.

The Adopted Home of Christ

"When Jesus heard that John had been put in prison, he withdrew to Galilee. Leaving Nazareth, he went and lived in Capernaum ..." (Matthew 4:12-13).

The city of Capernaum was located on the west shore of the beautiful Sea of Galilee, about two and a half miles south of where the Jordan River enters the lake. It was the adopted home of Jesus. He went to Capernaum following his rejection at the synagogue in Nazareth at the beginning of his public ministry. Capernaum was a teeming city of about 50,000 population. It was located on a main highway running from Damascus to Jerusalem. Quite possibly, the apostle Paul passed through the city prior to his experience on the way to Damascus. In all probability, there was a Roman military post located at Capernaum – a theory enhanced considerably by the experience Jesus had with the Roman centurion, an officer with 100 men under his command, concerning the centurion's slave.

Many are the experiences of Jesus related to Capernaum, which the Gospels reveal. It was here that Jesus called his first disciples – Peter and Andrew, two brothers of contrasting personalities. And James and John, also brothers and possibly partners with Peter and Andrew in the fishing business, were called by Jesus in this area. It was here also that Jesus called Matthew, the tax collector to discipleship. Quite possibly, Matthew had paid more than $20,000 for the right to tax in Capernaum. It was no small sum to give up in order to follow Christ. It was here in Capernaum that Jesus touched the hand of Peter's mother-in-law as she lay ill. The touch was followed by a loss of fever, and the lady arose and began to wait on her honored guest.

The fame of Jesus grew rapidly in and around Capernaum. Crowds flocked to see and hear this one who taught with authority and healed those who were sick. Once while Jesus was teaching and preaching in a house in the city, four men brought their paralyzed friend to Jesus to be healed. Unable to get into the house through the door, they carried their friend up the outside stairs to the roof. There they made a hole and lowered their friend down into the room where Jesus was. He was so impressed because of the persistent faith of the four men and had such great compassion for the paralyzed man that he healed him.

Very little remains of Capernaum today. Visitors can get only a thought of what the city must have been like in the days of Jesus from what the excavators have found. Possibly the best preserved structure is that of a second-century synagogue. Many believe these ruins are on the site of the synagogue where Jesus taught. A house excavated a short distance from that synagogue is thought to be, by some, the home of Peter. It is a possibility.

Capernaum was a city on the western shore of the Sea of Galilee. It was also the place where many were healed by Christ and many chose to follow him. In that respect, there are Capernaums located around the world.

Smile, Smile, Smile

Some years ago, several soldiers were having a good time in the soldiers' entertainment center. Someone began playing the piano, and a crowd gathered. Soon, the man playing the piano struck up a very familiar tune, and several in the crowd joined in singing. Some of you who are old enough may remember the song. It goes like this ... *What's the use of worrying? It never was worthwhile. So pack up your troubles in your old kit bag and smile, smile, smile.* Well, someone in the crowd recognized the man playing the piano. "Do you know who that is playing the piano?" he asked the soldier next to him. "That's Felix Lloyd Powell, the man who wrote the song."

You know, many wish life was as simple as the song suggests. It would be a neat trick if we could pack up our troubles in an old kit bag and spend a day smiling. But unfortunately, life doesn't operate that way. Some things in life cannot be tucked away and forgotten. It's true that many try to pack up their troubles. They try various bags. Some try the bag of alcohol, only to find that the trouble is still there when the hangover is gone. There's an old saying that the fastest way out of town is on a good, cheap drunk. The only catch is the town is still there when you wake up.

Still, others believe their troubles can be packed up in a dope needle. They try that bag. The only catch here is that the troubles won't stay in the bag unless we push another needle or eat another pill. And when we stop, those same troubles are still there looking us in the eye.

Police in Tacoma, Washington, found a note on the body of a 20-year-old well-dressed youth. In part, it said, "Dope ruined my life and took away my happiness forever. I could never live in a state of mind I was in." How we humans wish we could take a pill or push a button and our problems would be automatically solved.

Some years ago, a financially secure man told me that mankind was on the verge of building utopia here on earth by his own initiative. Then he said, "We can solve all our problems." One wonders sometimes if what we are building isn't closer to a Hades than a utopia. Unfortunately, you can't take a pill or push a button and get at the inside of a person. Life simply doesn't work that way.

But we can find help for our problems. God will help us. He may not lead us to a quick, easy, and simple solution, but he will help us. And when they get too heavy for us to carry, we can turn our troubles over to him. At least it will get the weight off of our back.

The music soon stopped in the soldiers' entertainment center. People went back to other things. In a few minutes, they heard a gunshot. Going to the room where the gunshot came from, they found Felix Lloyd Powell dead. There was a revolver in his hand.

Don't put your troubles in an old kit bag of any kind and continue smiling. If you can't handle them, turn them over to God. He can help.

Dropping Out of School

As a student at Emory University in Atlanta, I used to occasionally go down to the First Methodist Church to hear the minister, the late Pierce Harris, preach. For many years, Dr. Harris served the church as minister, and his Sunday evening services were attended by people from all over the country.

Dr. Harris once told a very dramatic and moving story about an incident which happened to him during his ministry. He was invited once to speak at a prison work camp. The prisoners were out in the open, and Dr. Harris had to speak from the bed of a truck. When it came time to introduce the speaker, one of the prisoners mounted the truck bed to make the introduction. The prisoner began his introduction by telling a story.

"Several years ago," he stated, "two boys lived in the same community of North Georgia. They attended the same school, played with the same bunch of boys, even went to the same Sunday school." The prisoner continued, "But one of the boys dropped out of the Sunday school because he felt he had outgrown it and that it was sissy stuff. The other boy kept going because he felt it was meaningful for his life."

You know, one stops at that point in the prisoner's introduction to do a little bit of thinking. What makes people drop out of Sunday school? I guess that the answer to that question is as varied as there are those who drop out, while often part of the reason is the way in which Sunday school is conducted. Most of the time it's due to a lack of interest on the part of the dropout and/or his parents. I guess many people don't value the worth of the Sunday school very much. If they did, they would stay with it even when it gets dry and dull, or even when it appears to be a little "sissy."

Another thing one thinks about is what causes people to go wrong, to break the laws of society by which people live. Again, one could say that sometimes the laws aren't just, and the prisoners are only victims. However, incidents of that nature are very, very few in number. In the vast majority of cases, the person sets himself above the law and ignores it. Of course, society has an influence on each person and the choices that he makes. But in the final analysis, each person chooses for himself the route his life will follow. He can choose to obey the law or to ignore it.

The prisoner on the bed of the truck concluded his introduction of Dr. Harris. "The boy who dropped out of Sunday school," the prisoner said, "stands before you today to introduce the speaker. The boy who stayed in Sunday school is the one who will speak."

Don't let anyone kid you. Your relationship to the church does have a very definite influence on the outcome of your life. Just remember this: Church business isn't sissy, kid stuff.

A Father's Prayer

Let me share with you a father's prayer that I wrote many, many years ago:

Dear God, I need your help to be the kind of father I should be. Hear my prayer. Help me, Father, to be more interested in the things my children are interested in. Too often, I find myself too deeply involved in my own thinking to pay much attention to what one of my children is saying. Remind me constantly that the things they're interested in are just as important as the things I am interested in. Help me to be a better listener.

Then, Father, help me to set aside some time in my busy schedule for the children. It seems that I'm always tied up with something, and even when I'm not, I think I'm too tired to spend some time in their activities.

Lord, help me keep my perspectives straight. Business can wait, but my children will only grow up once. Help me not to forget that children need love and attention as well as food and clothing while growing up. Too many times, I get so concerned about their material needs that I forget their emotional needs.

And Lord, I pray that my children will be able to see your love in me. If they can only see me living my faith, then they will understand it even if I can't put it in the right words for them. Help me to keep the important things important, and secondary things secondary. You know that many times the temptation is to neglect the important things of life while concentrating on secondary matters. Help me to teach kindness by being kind, forgiveness by forgiving, helpfulness by helping, and love by loving.

And dear God, help me prepare my children for marriage by being a good husband to their mother. If I'm a good husband, maybe it will help them when it comes time for them to take a life's partner. Help me to look for my children's good points and to brag on them a little more. You know, Lord, that I won't close my eyes to their faults. As their father, I must be able to see those, but, Lord, help me to dwell on their positive points. Another thing I will need your help in is having the power to say no to them when it should be said. We both know that many times a *no* is much better than a *yes*.

These children of mine are growing up, Lord. One day before long, they'll go out into the world on their own. They will choose an occupation. Help me to be man enough to rejoice in whatever they choose to do, and Christian enough to teach them that they can serve you in any occupation where they will work for the good of their fellow man.

Lord, I'm tempted to ask you to stop time to keep my children little children always. But I know that life doesn't operate that way, so I will just ask you to help me enjoy my children while they are children. Then in my old age, I will have beautiful memories of my children when they were small and be proud of them as adults.

Lord, I can't be a very good father without your help. So thanks for pitching in and giving me a helping hand. Amen.

Assembly Is Extra

Many years ago, I was in a department store and noticed several new bikes on display. Since Timmy had asked for a new 10-speed, I decided to look at them closer. I noticed the price tag on one of the bikes. Underneath the price, in very small print, was written *$5 extra if assembled.*

You know, I started thinking about that, about how much that extra little line applied to life. For life, you see, is like the bike; you have to pay extra to get it assembled. Life never comes assembled, even though we quite often wish it would. How easy it would be, we often think, if life came assembled in a neat package, ready for instant use. But the truth of the matter is that it doesn't. Each individual has to assemble his own life, to put it together himself. And like the bike in the store, we have to pay extra for the assembling. Now if the person who puts the bike together follows the directions that come with the package, that bike will provide years of service and withstand the bumps in the road over which it'll have to be ridden.

And you know, life is like that also. Put your life together following the manufacturer's guidelines, and you'll be able to meet the bumps in life's road without being damaged. Of course, if you pay no attention to either the instructions concerning the assembling of the bike or your life, you can expect trouble trying to make either operate correctly.

The man of Galilee gave us the clue when it comes to

putting our life together. Seek first God's way, he said, and the rest will fall in place. Despite many efforts, a better approach toward assembling life has never been found. We're given life but not as a finished product. We have to put some effort into it if it's ever to work right. You wouldn't dare take that box of unassembled bike parts, shake it real good, and expect the bike to fall out of the box completely assembled and ready to use. Why then should one expect life to fall into place automatically? It is extremely more delicate and has far more pieces to be fitted together than the bike. If your life seems to be hitting more and more bumps, which are becoming rougher and rougher, it is probably because you have failed to follow the instructions in attempting to assemble it.

You can, with your life as with the bike, reassemble it if it wasn't put together right to begin with. And it's foolish to think that your life will automatically correct itself any more than the bike will. You have to expend an effort and follow instructions if you expect your life or your bike to be ready to meet the rough places in the road.

Personally, I want my bike and my life to be able to take the bumps. For that reason, I try to follow the instructions given by my manufacturer, or Creator, as closely as I follow those off my bike's manufacturer. To me, it just makes good sense to do so.

I Saw God Today

I saw God today. Where did I see him, you ask? Well, I saw him in the face of a small child whose smile and laughter reminded me of the happiness and joy that comes from trusting a God who loves us.

I saw God today. Where did I see him, you ask? I saw him in the golden leaves of autumn, which fall each year and blossom each spring. I heard him in the rustling of the grass and in the song of a robin redbreast.

I saw God today. Where did I see him, you ask? I saw him in the person of a teacher who loved his students. I saw him struggling to teach so that the students could have a better life. I saw him toil alone in his labors, underpaid and often unappreciated.

I saw God today. Where did I see him, you ask? I saw him in the compassion of a doctor who was working with God to heal a patient. I saw him with his skills and knowledge as he helped relieve some of the suffering of a broken humanity.

I saw God today. Where did I see him, you ask? I saw him in the love of a father who was sweaty and tired from a hard day's work. I saw him work so that his family could have a house where they could make a home. I saw him work so that his children could get a good education. I saw him work so that the woman he loved could have a few of life's luxuries.

I saw God today. Where did I see him, you ask? I saw him in the person of a minister who wept with a family at the loss of a loved one, who rejoiced with a young couple at the birth of their first child, and who prayed for love, which he could pass on to those with whom he came in contact.

I saw God today. Where did I see him, you ask? I saw him in a public official who was elected to office by the people. I saw him as he tried to do his best in a society which often accepts and fosters crookedness. I saw him as he struggled to make a decision knowing that whatever decision he made would help some and hurt others, would be praised by some and condemned by others.

I saw God today. Where did I see him, you ask? I saw him in an ex-convict who is trying to make a new start in life. I saw him as his past life followed him everywhere he went. I saw him as he tried to start over, and no one was interested in giving him the chance.

I saw God today. Where did I see him, you ask? I saw him in a person – any person, every person – who reached out his hand to help another. I saw him as people overcame the differences of race and creed, education, status, in order that they could help one another.

I saw God today. Where did I see him, you ask? I saw him in the symbol of a cross. It reminded me of his great love for us. He loved us so much that he sent his only Son into our world to save us (John 3:16). His Son died for us, even when we weren't worth dying for. I saw him on the cross, and I heard his prayer of forgiveness for those who put him there.

So you see, I saw God today. You say you've never seen him? You can, my friend. If only you will look for him.

The Boy Who Would Write

Back during the first half of the 18th century, there was a young boy who aspired to be a writer. Because of his lack of formal education, the young boy wasn't sure of his ability. And his life had not been one that would foster self-confidence. His family had moved quite often, his father finally being jailed because of his inability to pay his debts. Because of the circumstances, this young boy had been able to attend school for only four years. To earn a living, he got a job putting labels on bottles of blacking in a dilapidated warehouse. He found him a place to sleep in a dismal attic, and he shared that room with others who couldn't afford anything better. But this young boy was determined to write.

And he did write, day after day. Finally, he got enough courage to submit a manuscript to a publisher. He mailed that manuscript at night when no one could see him because he was afraid someone might ridicule him. Soon he heard from the publisher. His manuscript was refused, rejected. Time and again, this young boy submitted his writings. Again and again, the same answer came back. Rejected! No publisher or paper was interested in his writings. But the desire to write was burning in the young boy's heart, and he refused to quit.

Finally, one of his stories was accepted. Now, he didn't receive any money for the story, but the editor did give him some praise. It was such a happy moment for him that he walked the streets with tears of joy coming down his cheeks.

Now, someone else had shown some belief in him. This bit of encouragement gave that young boy the impetus he needed to go on to greater things. And in a few years, all of England was reading his writings. The young boy believed in himself, believed he was capable of reaching the dream he had for himself in his heart. And for that reason, he would not quit.

You know, too often in life, we quit too soon. Many times, the victory is just around the corner, if we would only keep trying. It is of great importance that a person believes in himself. Selling ourselves short is no virtue. It is a vice. It hurts us. It keeps us from developing our God-given resources to become all that we can become, all that God wants us to become. The dreams we have for ourselves of what we can do and become can come true. They can, that is, if we are willing to continue to work toward the fulfillment of those dreams with all the resources we have. But we must remember that the fulfillment of any dream requires dedication, sacrifice, and persistence on our part.

Oh, incidentally, the young boy in London who refused to quit? His name? Charles Dickens. His novels are still read to this day. He believed in himself, so believe in yourself. God does.

Everyone Has Problems

Let me tell you something you already know. Everyone has problems. Now, we do not all have the same problems. But we do all have problems. No one goes sailing through life without hitting a high wave occasionally. Too often in our problems, we think other people turn their backs on us, and sometimes they do. But many times, it isn't that others turn their backs on us, it is simply that we have a defensive attitude, which causes us to expect others to reject us. In other words, we look for rejection on their part. We need to remember when we're in the midst of a problem that not near as many people know about it as we may think. Human capability is such that we don't know everything about every person at all times, and that is good.

It doesn't help to face our problems by being touchy about them either. I learned early in life that if you carried a chip on your shoulder, someone would try to knock it off. So I try to carry my chip in my back pocket, hidden from the view of those who get their kicks from knocking other people. I will share my problems with my close friends, who I know will try to help me understand, but I see no need to broadcast them to everyone I meet.

Don't become defensive if you happen to have problems that other people are aware of. Your defensiveness will often cause you to look for faults. Once I was visiting in a home where there were some problems. Several people in the town knew of those problems. A young boy in that home had run afoul of the law, and it had brought embarrassment to the family. As I was visiting, one of the parents remarked that they were in a certain place, and a person who they knew happened to be there. The parent of the young boy said that the other person didn't bother to speak. The parent thought, quite naturally, that the other person didn't speak because of the trouble the boy had had with the law and, obviously, felt hurt because of it. I then explained to the parent that the person who didn't speak probably didn't recognize the parent. That other person was probably concerned with the problems she had, which the parent wasn't aware of, but I knew of them. And the other person's problems were far more severe and serious. Yet very few people were even aware that that person who didn't speak even had any problem at all.

Don't follow your urge to become defensive when problems come your way. Don't wear your chip on your shoulder. Very few people will turn their backs on you because you have problems. And just remember that you aren't the only person in the world who has problems. We all do. Quite often, another person might have problems, which you know nothing about. Problems far more serious than yours. So when you have problems which others are aware of, don't become defensive. Just treat people as you would want them to treat you.

Two Basic Needs in Life

Every human has two basic needs when it comes to the area of love. One need is to love, and the other is to be loved. These are two basic needs of the human personality.

Once, while visiting in the hospital, I was stopped by an elderly lady in a wheelchair. She didn't know me, and I didn't know her, but she wanted to talk with someone. She told me about herself. She had no family to visit her, but some people from her church visited with her quite often. Tears came to her eyes as she told me about their visits. They meant so much to her. This elderly lady needed a little attention, some affection. Wanted to know someone cared for her, someone loved her.

We all have this need to be loved. To know that someone cares for us, to know that we are important to someone. It's a hunger in the human heart to be loved. It's a natural hunger, as natural as breathing. Then also every person needs to give love. Robert Hugh Benson once said, "It is only the souls that do not love that go empty in this world." Give love, and love will be given you. Not always by all those you give love to, and not always in the manner you desire, but by enough people to make life enjoyable.

Now, I'm not a psychologist, but I've seen enough of life to know that love must have an outlet. Unexpressed love can be extremely dangerous to the human personality. I've even seen unexpressed love turn to hatred. A home where love is given and received by all members of the family is a happy home. A home where one member, only one member, fails to give or receive love is often a miserable experience.

So I say again, love must have an outlet. I've seen couples who did not have any children love a pet as they would a child. Why? Because of the need to express love. Children are part of God's plan to give parents an outlet to express love. So are our marriage partners. They are a part of God's practical plan to help us meet this need. It's just as important to learn to accept love as it is to give love. However, you can accept love without giving. But I don't think you can give love without accepting. Therefore, the emphasis should be on giving.

Now, these two basic human needs must be met vertically as well as horizontally. We need to love God and accept God's love of us. The best way we can express our love for God is to love our fellow man. An unknown author has put it this way: "I sought my soul, but my soul I could not see. I sought my God, but my God eluded me. I sought my brother and found all three."

Each of us has two basic needs: to love and to be loved. Remember to give love, and love will be given to you. Accept God's love, and love him in return. If you will learn to do these things, life will be enjoyable and worth the effort it takes to live.

Faith. Yes, Faith.

Faith. Yes, faith. How much that word has shaped our world. How many lives have grown into personhood because of faith? What is faith? A man answered that question 2,000 years ago. He said that faith is the assurance that something we want will come to pass. He said that faith is to be certain of things which we can't even see (Hebrews 11:1). Faith is when one dares to go farther then he can see, to be willing to trust without any evidence that he should trust.

How much faith does a person need? Well, that question also has been answered. It was answered by a Galilean carpenter as he stood on the Mount of Olives and taught his disciples. He said if we had "faith as small as a mustard seed," that it would be enough to work miracles (Matthew 17:20).

What has faith done for people? Well, it's put a song in their hearts. It has brought sight to their eyes. It has put movement into their muscles and joy into their lives. Faith has founded empires. It has established principles. It has changed the world. Those who have accomplished the most for mankind have been people of faith.

Faith. Faith in whom? *Faith in God*, first of all, for he's the author of faith, and without faith in him, all else loses its high purpose. *Faith in ourselves*, next. This, too, is of utmost importance, and if you have faith that you can, then you'll find a way, and the whole world can't stop you. And *faith, also, in our fellow man*. This faith will be shaken often and even broken at times, but you must never lose it. Because if faith in your fellow man dies, then your hope for a better world dies also. Above all, remember that God has faith in you. That's the reason behind the cross. That's the purpose of the empty tomb. He has faith that you will choose the highest, the best, the purest.

Don't ever lose this wonderful thing we call faith. For life is dull and void and ugly without it. So keep faith in God, in yourself, and in your fellow man. Faith will pull you up when you're down. Faith will heal your wounds when you're hurt. Faith will help you extend a helping hand to a brother who has wronged you, and faith will heal the sickness in your heart. Seek out faith, find her, pay whatever price is asked for her, and let her be your constant companion on the road of life. She'll make you richer than all the money the world has.

What Is It You Really Want?

In life, a person should be sure that what he's working toward is what he wants. Too many times, a person spends his life working toward a goal. And then when he reaches the goal, discovers that he didn't really want what he got. Marjorie Merriweather Post, who was sometimes referred to as Grande Dame Post, spent much of her 86 years climbing society's ladder.

She became one of the nation's leading society queens. However, toward the end of her life, she expressed regrets at having spent so much time at the top. At one of the last parties she held, while surrounded by gushing women, she leaned over to a friend and confided: "To think I worked 50 years just to have these [and she called the ladies present a name] bow and scrape to me."

One of the cruel tricks which life plays on us is to give us that which we ask for. And many times, we discover that the more we get of what we want, the less we want of what we get. In ancient Greek mythology, there was a story of Midas. Midas had done the gods a favor, and his reward was that any one wish he had would be fulfilled. Midas wished that everything he touched would turn to gold. Well, his wish was fulfilled, but he nearly starved to death before he got it changed.

Some time ago, there was a special program on television about several bright young executives who were apparently on their way up in the business world. The report told how one by one they had turned their backs on the climb to the top and accepted jobs paying much less. The more they got of what they wanted, the less they wanted of what they got. A person should be sure, before he sets out working toward something, that what he is working toward is what he wants. For the chances are pretty good that he'll get what he wants. To me, the most terrible frustration life could give would be to spend your whole life in pursuit of something and then when you finally get it, discover that it wasn't worth pursuing at all.

I remember reading a story about a restless young boy who wanted to be free, away from the restraints and restrictions of his father. So he left home one day in a sullen mood and headed toward a place where he could do as he pleased. But the story went on to point out that the more he did of what he wanted, the less he wanted to do what he did. And then one day, he came back home to do something worthwhile, to be the son of his father (Luke 15:11-31). Make sure that what you're working for in life is worth working for. Give it close examination before you decide to invest your life pursuing it. Weigh it on the scales of life. Compare it with the virtues of love and service.

Don't waste your life in pursuit of that which you do not want. I know few disappointments in life that would be more crushing than working for something and getting it, only to discover it wasn't really what you wanted at all.